96'

THE BUSINESS OF CRIME

Robert Rice

THE BUSINESS O[

Farrar, Straus & Cudahy   New York

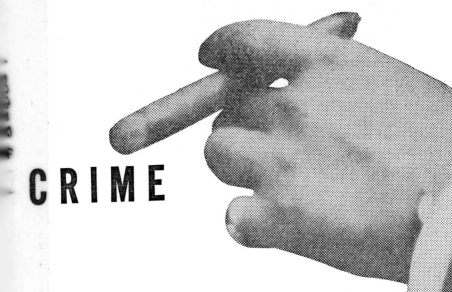

CRIME

18141

The articles "Sam Sapphire" (originally published
under the title "Torch in Brooklyn") and "Salvatore
Sollazzo" (originally published under the title
"The Bewildered Fixer") first appeared, in slightly
different form, in The New Yorker and were copyrighted
in 1950 and 1955, respectively by the The New Yorker
Magazine, Inc.
Published simultaneously in Canada by Ambassador
Books, Ltd., Toronto. Manufactured in the United
States of America by H. Wolff, New York
Library of Congress catalog card number 56–9444
DESIGN : Marshall Lee

First Printing, 1956

Author's note

In many instances I have invented fictitious names for the characters
in this book; in many instances I have used real names. It would be im-
possibly tedious to list in detail which people are traveling incognito. It
suffices to state that I have used an alias whenever it has seemed to me
that a relatively blameless person has somehow become involved with the
assorted crooks with whom this book deals, or whenever I have felt that
a crook, however heinous his behavior, has already been adequately—
or, in a number of cases, excessively—punished for it.

It would have been clearly impossible to gather more than a fraction
of the material that appears in these pages without the active and un-
stinting cooperation of dozens of policemen, government officials, attorneys, corporation executives and private citizens in all walks of life. I
am especially indebted to Bruce Bielaski of the National Board of Fire
Underwriters; Harry J. Anslinger, United States Commissioner of Narcotics; the Messrs. J. K. Livingston and Norman F. Page of the American
Express Company; U. E. Baughman, Chief of the United States Secret
Service; Frank Hogan, District Attorney of New York County, and his
former assistant, now Commissioner of Marine and Aviation, Vincent A. J.
O'Conor; and Raymond F. Farrell, Assistant Commissioner, Investigations
Division, Immigration and Naturalization Service of the United States
Department of Justice.

Finally, I want to thank William Shawn, editor of The New Yorker,
and Joseph Kastner, for their priceless editorial advice.

contents

PART ONE
Sam Sapphire

PART TWO
Elias Eliopoulos

PART THREE
The Counterfeiters

PART FOUR
Jorge Gregorio Simonovich

The argument of this book

Crime, heaven knows, is not an underpublicized phenomenon. There is no telling how many square miles of virgin forest are felled each year to edify the readers of murder mysteries, true-detective magazines and mass circulation newspapers. Figures are painstakingly compiled on the average number of larcenies per cubic foot in mid-western cities of between fifty and seventy-five thousand population; learned papers are published in scientific journals on the relationship between arson and the id; "public enemies" are as carefully ranked as guests at a diplomatic dinner party. Acute as the problem of crime in our society may be, it would be unforgivable to add even one word to this spate without a pretty firm conviction that that word had not yet been emphatically enough said. The good many more words than one that appear between these covers are the fruit of a long-standing notion that one particularly pervasive and influential kind of crime receives particularly little public notice. It is the kind that is a natural and inevitable part of the human activity known as "business" —or, in the native tongue of some of its less elegant practitioners, "making a buck." It is the most uncomfortable kind to discuss, or even describe, because it involves grasping the thorny fact that for many people—only some of whom are crooks—"business" is not just a way to make a living but a way of life, not just a vocation but a *mystique*.

As the word is used here, "business" is any occupation whose sole object is making money. The notion that making money is, per se, a sufficient purpose in life is patently an arbitrary, not to say metaphysical one, and it gives rise to a unique moral code. The words "good" and "bad" take on special meanings in connection with business. If money can be made from shoes, then shoes are "good"; if it can't be made from ships, ships are "bad." Such questions as whether or not shoes are more useful than ships, or, for that matter, whether or not the shoes are durable, comfortable or attractive shoes, are quite beside the point except insofar as they throw light on how money is to be gotten. The ordinary spectacle of the honorable, kind-hearted, philanthropic businessman who conscientiously underpays his employees is one that can only mean that the morality of business is not necessarily the morality of anything else. The renowned law of supply and demand, even, is really an exercise in metaphysics. There is no divine ordinance stating that scarce goods must be expensive, or that whatever someone wants must be provided to him. Such a "law" is simply a development of the unprovable—and, at the same time, irrefutable—first premise that money-making is constructive work. Being what it is, therefore, business morality is bound to come into frequent conflict with moralities of various other kinds, and some of the time it is bound to triumph over them. A high proportion of the famous laws of the twentieth century—the Hepburn Act, the Clayton anti-trust law, the various food and drug acts, to name only a few—were written because it was plain enough for any congressman to see that what was good for business was often the exact reverse of good for the country. For a sufficiently dedicated business moralist it is surely only a short step from not caring whether he concerns himself with shoes or ships to not caring whether he concerns himself with shoes or ships or heroin; in fact to believing, as did Elias Eliopoulos, whose career is discussed at length later, that heroin is "good." "Making a buck" is often augmented by those who use the phrase into "making an honest buck," but the adjective is redundant. A true believer knows that honest is the only kind of buck there is.

The idea that one common sort of criminal is a faithful worshiper of the same god whom many an honest man adores is not, of course, terribly popular with honest men. It is much more convenient to consider crime—in a word, evil—in its timeless aspects rather than in its timely ones. Crime is easiest to understand—and condemn—when it imitates art, not business, and so accounts of crime are likely to be a substitute for fiction if they aren't fiction to begin with. The police reports in any day's newspaper will turn up half a dozen serviceable plots for novels about good and evil, but one must turn to the political or financial news to learn much about crime in the United States of America in the year 1956. It is true that crime is eternal, that the deadly sins are always with us, that every age has its Othellos and Lady Macbeths, its Cains, Oedipuses and Fausts. The fate of such outsize characters though, is in the lap of God, not Congress or the safe and loft squad, and the definitive, if by no means the last, laws affecting such people were enacted several thousand years ago on top of Mount Sinai. Most crime consists of breaking laws that even the most determined evangelist would have to

admit are Caesar's, not God's. It is timely, workaday, un-
dramatic. It is committed casually and without qualms by
commonplace people under commonplace circumstances.
It is an outgrowth of, or an effort to live with, booms and
busts, political and technological revolutions, and hot and
cold wars. It is as integral a part of man's eternally hope-
ful, eternally frustrating attempt to lead the good life as
any other widely practiced human activity. There may be
a person who has never exceeded a speed limit, patronized
a speakeasy, ordered theater tickets from a speculator,
fudged an income-tax return, let a dog run loose, committed adultery, sneaked a piece of jewelry past Customs,
bought a package of black-market cigarettes, kept a business open on Sunday, placed a bet with a bookmaker, lib-
erated a German camera, shot a deer out of season, given a
Christmas present to a policeman, slipped a roll of bills under the table to a landlord, overstated damages to an insurance company or used obscene language in a public
place. If there is, he is not easy to find, and once he is
found he may very well turn out to be the fellow who, in
despair over his wasted life, has just chopped up his wife
and children with a dull hatchet.

The foregoing enumeration—an extremely brief one in
relation to the number of laws on the books—is not intended to suggest that everyone under the sun is a criminal, but simply that anyone under the sun could be. It
illustrates the obvious fact that in our extraordinarily complicated world a criminal is not an easy person to identify.
It is fairly clear that someone who now and then performs
one of the deeds on that list cannot seriously be regarded
as a criminal. It is just as clear that someone who repeatedly performs all of them is a criminal of the deepest dye.
That leaves Congress, the safe and loft squad, and all the

rest of us, squarely confronting the sticky question of how often who has to do what to qualify as a bona fide crook. In our efforts to answer it, we are seriously disadvantaged by our disposition to believe that the Criminal is somehow different from the Man. We profess to have outgrown Lombroso's notion that there is such a thing as a "criminal type," and we quote voluminous, and accurate, statistics that establish for instance, that in such matters as cranial formation, mechanical aptitude, blood pressure, reasoning powers, endocrine function and religious impulses the prison population of the United States is a pretty representative cross section of the general population. But in the next breath we talk about criminals being "disturbed personalities," a cant phrase which, at best, updates Lombroso by implying that a man's misdeeds are his parents' fault instead of his own, at worst, puts a primitive Calvinist thought into the opaque language of the New Criticism, and, in either event, merely repeats the ancient solecism that a crook is a crook is a crook.

Actually a crook is a crook is a crook only in the dictionary, where he is defined as "one who has been found guilty of a crime." In characterizing specific individuals, accurate usage, common decency and the libel laws all oblige one to pay attention to Webster. However, any definition that in nine words, eight of them monosyllables, is able to effectively blanket such assorted personalities as John Dillinger, Harry K. Thaw, Loeb and Leopold, Waxey Gordon, Robert Whitney, Willie Sutton, Lizzie Borden and Robin Hood is pretty primitive, and it is no more enlightening than the observation that whales, giraffes, two-toed sloths and disc jockeys are all mammals, or that quail, deliquescence, pique and cumquat are all common nouns containing the letter "q." Besides being a crook, a crook might also be a plumber, a husband, a peeping Tom, a stamp collector, a Venezuelan, a blonde, a stockholder or almost anything else, and some of the other things that he is may have a good deal to do with his crookedness. He is very often a businessman, and it is in that capacity that he is described in this book. The specific respects in which, when he is a businessman, a crook isn't just any old crook are therefore worth exploration.

One extremely significant fact about the businessman-crook is that he can survive in our society a good deal more easily than most other criminals because he has considerably more moral standing. The income-tax evader, say, or the black marketer or the bucket-shop operator is too close a relative of too many of us to be regarded with the horror that a criminal theoretically deserves. Most members of civilized society are taught from the cradle up to employ caution and control in the expression of pride, lust, anger, gluttony, envy and sloth—in fact all but one of the deadly passions—and so it is natural for us to be immediately and genuinely outraged by the deeds of Jack the Ripper, Pretty Boy Floyd, or, for that matter, any minor wife beater or mugger. We are also taught from the cradle up that the more or less unbridled expressions of the acquisitive instinct is not only normal but socially constructive; a substantial part of our everyday economic behavior is squarely founded on the unprecedented theory that covetousness makes the world go round, and so our indignation is perplexed and diluted by self-consciousness when we are confronted with the Teapot Dome deal or a ten percenter. If we got wind of a conspiracy to hold up a bank, most of us automatically holler, "Help! Police!" But if we get wind of a conspiracy to sell merchandise at a discount in violation of a fair trade law, few of us do.

As a matter of fact, public complicity in business crime is not only moral and psychological; it is physical as well. An essential chracteristic of business is that it is a social activity. There can be no sellers without buyers, whether the goods offered for sale are sewing machines or stolen rubies. Each one of us, at one time or another, has a need, real or fancied, for some commodity or service that is impossible to get legally: a package of cigarettes, a three-and-a-half room apartment, a paving contract, an abortion. It is obviously quite difficult for us to treat the businessman who sells whatever it is we want as a criminal unless we are willing to treat ourselves as criminals too. Herein, undoubtedly, lies the unique character—and danger—of business crime. When young Howard Unruh sallied into a street in Camden, New Jersey, and shot down the first sixteen passersby he saw, when a gang of teenagers kicked an old bum to death and rolled him into the East River, when John Dillinger shot it out with the FBI, when an armed gang hijacked the Brink's armored truck, they were on their own. They originated their crimes and the public was not implicated in them except to the extent that each of us has had an occasional fantasy in which we too struck out at the world in blind or calculated rage. The criminals described in this book played an entirely different social role. Each one of them implicated dozens, in some cases hundreds, of "honest men," if, in fact, it wasn't the "honest men" who implicated them. Sam Sapphire could not have been an arsonist if there had not been a large number of respectable citizens ready and able to purchase an arsonist's services. Jorge Simonovich's travel bureau was organized for the benefit of aliens willing to enter the United States illegally. Salvatore Sollazzo could not have corrupted college basketball players if college basketball players hadn't been corruptible—or, more likely, already partly corrupted by college admissions authorities and loyal alumni. Lord knows the argument is a familiar one: Horse parlors can't exist without bettors, houses of prostitution without prurient males, speakeasies without drinkers, opium dens without narcotics addicts. Three cheers for the law of supply and demand. The mightiest law of all!

Finally, a word should be said about the relationship between crime and violence, and how that relationship affects business crime. Beyond question one reason that business crime is less shocking than some other kind is that violence is an incidental or accidental, rather than an integral part of it, a means not an end. A code of values that holds that the taking of one human life is of more consequence than the taking of however many dollars you care to name is eminently defensible and so, from an emotional standpoint, it is quite appropriate that Al Capone, as a folk villain, is the malevolent savage who organized the St. Valentine's Day massacre rather than the able businessman who organized the Chicago bootlegging trade. (It is interesting to note, incidentally, that Capone owes his status as a dictionary "criminal" to income-tax evasion, a business crime if there ever was one.) When, in other words, violence is part of business crime, the violence generally obscures the business in the public mind, and when it isn't —which is quite often since, it is safe to say, many men intellectually and psychologically capable of managing a large and complicated conspiracy are too well adjusted to resort to violence unless they have to—the crime itself does not have nearly the emotional appeal of an axe murder or a kidnapping. However, if Al Capone's violence is regarded from, as it were, the inside rather than the outside, a curious sight is to be seen. Under a flagrantly different external shape, it is apparently the same basic tool that legitimate businessmen use every day: the law. From one standpoint, after all, the law also is violence, petrified violence, to be sure, violence caught in amber, but violence nevertheless. Law is enforceable only insofar as armed policemen are waiting in the stationhouse; they may never be called out, but their presence is implied every time a judge writes a decision, or a legislature enacts a bill. Resorting to law is a technique every businessman uses to prevent his competitors or associates from doing him in. It is a technique, obviously, a criminal can't use. And so, instead of calling a lawyer, he calls a strong-arm man. In short, when a business criminal resorts to violence he is still doing business.

The five conspiracies described in the ensuing sections of this volume concern, in the main, the crimes of arson, selling narcotics, counterfeiting, smuggling (both people and things) and gambling. Obviously, therefore, they were not chosen as being literally typical of the kind of crime ordinarily committed by businessmen—although they do peripherally involve black-marketing, corruption of public officials, tax fraud and various other familiar and representative business crimes. As a matter of fact they were chosen precisely because they were not typical. Although each one of the conspiracies involved illegal actions that are popularly regarded—whether with or without justification—as much more heinous than those that businessmen usually indulge in, each one, alarmingly enough, was contrived by bona fide businessmen, each one used the accustomed tools and techniques of business, and each one was animated by the profound and unalterable business conviction that man was put on this earth to make a dollar. The spirit of free enterprise, it would appear, is quite capable of inspiring almost any kind of crime.

There is one other respect in which these otherwise totally unlike conspiracies are similar. Each one, in a real sense, sprang from the convolutions and convulsions of the twentieth century world. Sam Sapphire's Brooklyn arson plot sprang from the Great Depression which made insurance money the most likely source of revenue for a large number of small businessmen. Elias Eliopoulos's vast international narcotics business was a curious illustration of a familiar One World thesis: What made Eliopoulos a rich man was the jealous regard for its national sovereignty that consumed each of the countries in which he operated; as soon as the League of Nations was able to instigate a small degree of international cooperation among law-enforcement officers, Eliopoulos was undone. (It is singular that policemen, in this instance at least, should be so much more sensible than statesmen; it is thirty years or more ago that a minor horror like the narcotics traffic inspired governments to work together, but one looks in vain for the day when war, the most aggravated kind of criminal behavior there is, will have the same effect on them.) The motley group responsible for counterfeiting American Express Company traveler's cheques in Paris just after the end of the Second World War was provided with political inspiration by the activities of the Palestine terrorists; with economic opportunity by the post-war black market, and with technical know-how by its experience during the Resistance. Jorge Simonovich's immigrant-smuggling trade was the direct result of the war's gigantic displacement of persons, and it owed a great part of its success to one of the notable technological triumphs of our time, the coming of age of the airplane. The hapless Salvatore Sollazzo was speeded along the path to perdition by the "soft" status of the currency in most countries of the world—although it is questionable whether he could have told you what a soft currency was—and by the odd circumstance that many respected figures of the world of higher education apparently regard a winning basketball team as worth almost any moral price.

The author of this book is, by inclination, by training and by trade, an author and nothing more. His accounts of and comments on crime are reportorial and, conceivably, literary. He has no "solution" for the crime problem, no observations about the nature of the criminal mind, no code of laws, scheme of prison reform or recommendations about parole procedure to offer. He is venturesome enough to write on this extremely difficult subject because of his reportorial and, conceivably, literary conviction that all too often in our society the moral difference between a businessman and criminal is imperceptible. If that is true, if much crime is, indeed, conventional, not eccentric, behavior, surely the fact is worth recording.

PART ONE

Sam Sapphire

1 *Sam the inside man*

The Borough of Brooklyn in the years 1930, 1931 and 1932 enjoyed a normal rainfall. It was struck by lightning no more often than usual. The Fordham University seismograph reported no temblors there, nor was there any evidence of volcanic activity between Williamsburg and the sea. There is no reason to believe that, during those years, more than the customary number of nonchalant citizens abandoned oily rags in unventilated corners, dozed off clutching lighted cigars, or overloaded their electric circuits. Among small children playing with matches remained a popular diversion, but one that by no means reached epidemic proportions. The fact is, nevertheless, that Brooklyn in the years 1930, 1931 and 1932 was a singularly inflammable community. Not since the eighteen-seventies had fires been such a familiar feature of daily life there. In 1932 the Brooklyn companies of the New York City Fire Department responded to 15,817 calls compared with 10,181 in 1928 and 12,455 in 1929, and losses paid to burned-out Brooklynites by fire insurance companies that year amounted to almost eight million dollars as against some five million in 1928 and six million in 1929. Toward the end of the year several companies were seriously considering refusing to write any more policies on Brooklyn property.

It would be an unmerited slur upon the acumen of the fire prevention authorities to imply that Brooklyn's sudden inflammability surprised them. 1930, 1931 and 1932 were, as the eighteen-seventies had been, years of economic crisis. In such years one of the most popular methods of eluding bankruptcy is to collect fire insurance. Legal papers drawn in Brooklyn in 1930, 1931 and 1932 continued to describe fire as an act of God, but to a number of cynical observers in the offices of the Police Commissioner, the Fire Marshal, the Kings County District Attorney and the National Board of Fire Underwriters it seemed probable that the Lord was getting a good deal of unsolicited help. Of all these cynics, none were more exasperated by the thought that Brooklyn had become the site of a large and lucrative plot to destroy property by fire than the detectives employed by the Arson Department of the National Board of Fire Underwriters. The National Board is an association of almost all the capital stock fire insurance companies in the nation; its members write about eighty-five percent of the fire policies written in the United States; its purpose is to act as the arm of the trade in such matters, among others, as compiling statistics, developing safety engineering techniques, handling public relations, and helping public officials apprehend citizens who find it either profitable or entertaining to burn things up. It is with the last named activity, of course, that the Arson Department is concerned, and because, to the members of the National Board, arson is a matter of large amounts of money, the department commands resources of cash and manpower that are the envy of tightly budgeted official investigators. Fires in Brooklyn in 1930, 1931 and 1932 were costing National Board members over a million dollars a year more than they were taking in from that borough, and so the department felt justified in instituting an all-out investigation. It got under way in the fall of 1932, in cooperation with the offices of the New York City Fire Marshal and the Kings County District Attorney. It took six months and several thousand dollars to complete. Like any inquiry into an extensive, loosely organized criminal conspiracy, it developed numerous false trails and cul-de-sacs, it involved long periods of patient waiting, and it depended partly on luck. By the time it was all over, though, twenty-six people had been convicted of arson, including a man who, between October, 1931, and May, 1933, had set upward of a hundred fires, at a cost to the insurance companies of nearly half a million dollars. In 1933, the years in which he and twenty-five fellow workers were rounded up, fire claims paid in Brooklyn declined by four million dollars.

The head of the Arson Department in 1932 was a large, hearty connoisseur of criminals named Alexander Bruce Bielaski, who had been a practising detective almost continuously since his graduation from law school in 1904. His first job, after leaving school, was with the Bureau of Investigation, predecessor in the United States Justice Department to the FBI. Between 1908 and 1918 he was in charge of the Bureau's checkup on pro-German activities in the United States. He resigned after the end of the First World War and set up a law office in Manhattan, but even so he apparently could not avoid involvement with criminals. In 1922, while taking a trip through Mexico, he was kidnapped by bandits and held for ransom. After three days of captivity he escaped. In 1925 he was appointed a special assistant to the U.S. Attorney General to prosecute liquor smugglers in New York. Since 1929 he has been with the National Board of Fire Underwriters, making things uncomfortable for people who burn up insured property.

To Bielaski's experienced eye the profusion of fires in Brooklyn in 1932 was by no means the only visible sign that crooks were at work there. Every week at least a couple of Brooklyn fires started, according to the fire department, from "cause unknown"; occurred in the stores, factories or homes of small businessmen known to be in financial straits; were of the handy variety that made the contents of a store, home or factory a total insurance loss without seriously damaging the premises themselves; and were seldom a threat to the personal safety of the buildings' inhabitants since, by a rather suspicious clairvoyance, the tenants of such buildings almost always managed to be off the premises when the fires began—which was often four in the morning. Bielaski decided that his first move should be to send an "inside man" into Brooklyn, "inside man" being the technical term for an operative who has the curious trait of being willing and able to affiliate himself with criminals and work his way into their confidence. The inside man Bielaski selected for this mission was a short, bald, guilty-looking Hungarian who spoke not only his native tongue and English, but also Polish, Russian, Rumanian, German and Yiddish, and who had become proficient in boring from within while rounding up reds for A. Mitchell Palmer, bootleggers for Mabel Walker Willebrandt and dope peddlers for the United States Treasury Department. The pseudonym he used on the Brooklyn job was Sam Samuels. For Samuels's point of entry into the Brooklyn underworld Bielaski chose the block between Avenue W and Gravesend Road on Mansfield Place, an undistinguished thoroughfare out near Sheepshead Bay. Samuels found an apartment there in November, and promptly moved in.

Bielaski's choice of that Mansfield Place block was by no means random; during the previous spring and summer there had been half a dozen fires of a questionable nature in apartments there. The most interesting thing about these fires was that in each of them the left sleeve and shoulder of a black sealskin coat, size 44, had been burned away. Adjusters for the various insurance companies involved felt—and Bielaski heartily agreed—that in a block which contained six size 44 ladies with identically damaged black sealskin coats, the law of averages was not the only law that was being flouted. Samuels never did solve the sealskin coat fires which had been, apparently, a sort of small family affair, but he did deviously come across much larger game.

In much of his work Samuels was accustomed to receive help from his wife, who continued to live in their real home, several miles from Mansfield Place, but who spent a certain amount of time with him in the role of a girl friend. (Samuels had discovered that the more rakish he could make himself out to be, the better he got along with his quarries.) The Samuelses often took prolonged strolls through the neighborhood, stopping in this store or that to make small purchases and converse with the proprietors. One evening, a week or two after he had established himself, he and Mrs. Samuels walked into a drygoods store on Mermaid Avenue in Coney Island to buy a pair of curtains for a bathroom window. Mrs. Samuels, a handsome young woman with an agreeable gift for small talk, remarked to the storekeeper that he seemed to have a nice little business there. "Nice!" said the storekeeper. "Believe me, it should burn."

"Why, what do you mean?" said Mrs. Samuels.

"What do I mean?" said the storekeeper. "I mean business is so rotten, I should listen to my friends and have a fire."

"But you can't do a thing like that," said Mrs. Samuels.

"Who can't?" said the storekeeper. "People are doing it every day."

"Do you mean it?" said Samuels, his normally guilty expression becoming positively conspiratorial.

"Listen," said the storekeeper, "I got a friend, he knows the best *macher* in the business. I give my friend a couple hundred, I go home some night, next morning no more store."

"What's that, a *macher*?" said Samuels.

"*Borey m'orey ha-ash*," said the storekeeper, repeating a phrase from a Hebrew prayer that means "He who creates the light of fire." He winked.

Samuels winked back. "Listen," he said, "I got a brother-in-law, he's got a factory in New York, it's in trouble. All the time he's saying to me, 'I got to have a fire, but I don't know how.' What's your friend's name? Maybe I could help my brother-in-law out."

"Abe Davidoff," said the storekeeper, and he gave Samuels a telephone number where Davidoff could be reached.

"You're sure this Davidoff's *macher* is a reliable man," Samuels said.

"The best in the business," said the storekeeper. "I'll tell you, you walk down the block and look at the stationery store on the corner. Abe fixed that one last week. What an explosion!"

Mrs. Samuels paid for the curtains, and she and her husband left the store. When they got to the corner they stopped to look at the stationery store. The front of it was boarded up, the exterior was charred, and, as far as they could see by peering through a crack, the store had been completely gutted. When Samuels got back to Mansfield Place he called Davidoff, introduced himself as a friend of the storekeeper's and described his imaginary brother-in-law, who, he said had a factory, devoted to the manufacture of children's hats and caps, that was losing money. Davidoff seemed delighted at the news. "How much insurance your brother-in-law's got?" he said.

"Please," said Samuels, "not on the telephone."

"I'll see you tomorrow morning," Davidoff said. Samuels gave him the Mansfield Place address. The next morning Davidoff showed up. He was a stout, seedy-looking, elderly man with a red face and a habit of rubbing his hands together. Despite his unprepossessing appearance, however, Samuels found in his personality a certain attractive wistfulness. He was a trustful soul. He had been a woolens manufacturer who had gone bankrupt in 1925, and he was now selling fire insurance, although he had no broker's license. With each policy he issued a guarantee that the sale would be followed shortly by a fire. "I'm just trying to make an honest dollar," he often said.

Samuels and Davidoff became buddies almost immediately, a relationship that owed a good deal to Samuels's expense account, which was elastic. During his operations in Brooklyn, Samuels drew from a hundred to a hundred and fifty dollars a week in expenses, and a good part of these funds was spent in purchasing food and drink for Davidoff, whose appetite for both far outstripped his ability to pay for them. The two met almost daily to try to arrange the fire in the hat factory on Seventeenth Street, on which Samuels said his brother-in-law carried $18,000 insurance. There really was a hat factory on Seventeenth Street, belonging to a friend of Samuels, and Samuels showed Davidoff around it one afternoon. The role Samuels played in these negotiations, which stretched out interminably, was that of a pessimistic fellow who didn't believe that Davidoff's *macher*—a term that Samuels translated as "mechanic" in his written reports to Bielaski—could do a good job, and who didn't think even a good job was worth five hundred dollars, the price Davidoff set. Davidoff, his professional integrity thus challenged, outdid himself as a salesman. A typical excerpt from one of Samuels's reports follows:

"Davidoff suggested stopping some place for a drink. We proceeded to a speakeasy on the southeast corner of Christie and Broome streets, where we stayed some time discussing the intended fire. Operative then took subject to his apartment where a few more drinks were consumed. A couple of ladies, friends of subject, joined the party. The ladies left at midnight but subject stayed over. Subject disclosed a number of jobs that he engineered in the past few months, mentioning an ice cream parlor at ——Street and——Avenue, Borough Park, Brooklyn; name of the owner is Bernstein; the owner, Mrs. Bernstein, originally contracted with one G——to have the place burned, and was going to pay him $500—$200 cash and $300 in notes. Subject learned of the intended job through a friend of his and he (Davidoff) offered to do the job for $300 cash, which he did. It was recently learned that G—— is sort of sore because of being cheated out of some easy money. Subject continually boasted of his good standing with several politicians and, in particular, with his adjuster, whose name is Sam and who is president of the Borough Hall Boys' Association and whose partner is a former fire marshal; that the adjusters are in with him on the deals and that he guarantees every job to be perfect. He remarked that it was a coincidence that the name of his mechanic was Sam, the first name of the adjuster was Sam and the first name of operative is also Sam, and that this would make a good combination." Bielaski was pleased to receive the news of the two additional Sams. Davidoff, after all, was not much of a menace, maybe twenty or twenty-five thousand dollars worth a year, but Sam the adjuster and Sam the *macher* sounded like the million-dollar babies he was looking for.

² Sam the adjuster

The first of the added Sams that Samuels reported on was by no means a new Sam to Bielaski. Davidoff's description of him made it clear that he was a well-known man-about-Brooklyn whose career Bielaski had been pondering over for a year or more, and whose name will here be given as Samuel Berliner. Berliner was a member of the extremely successful Brooklyn firm of Reilly & Berliner, public adjusters. A public adjuster is a man, licensed by the state, whose business is representing the victims of fires in dealing with insurance companies; in return for his skill at prying every possible dollar from underwriters, he generally receives ten percent of the sum recovered. The senior partner in Reilly & Berliner was Vincent Joseph Reilly, once an assistant fire marshal. He had left that position to join the distinguished old public adjusting firm of O'Toole, McClanahan & Co., of which he became treasurer. O'Toole, McClanahan was a firm with a fine reputation. O'Toole was a brother of a former Kings County sheriff and McClanahan was a brother of a former county register. The two founders were elderly gentlemen when Reilly joined them, and the burden of day-to-day operations was borne by Reilly, who as an ex-assistant fire marshal was well acquainted with the fire department's operations and personnel. In 1831 Reilly induced Berliner to join O'Toole, McClanahan. Berliner was thirty-eight years old and an ex-grand jury foreman. Most of his life had been devoted to the astute management of a sporting goods store in downtown Brooklyn. In 1929 he had sold the store at a good profit and bought a restaurant in the same neighborhood. Since Berliner had been a founder, and was president, of an influential political club, the Borough Hall Boys, to which a number of judges, assistant district attorneys and other public servants adhered, his restaurant had rapidly become a rendezvous for the statesmen who made Borough Hall the center of their activities. Early in 1931 a friend of his, a public adjuster, told him that a man with as many significant acquaintances as he had could make his fortune in the public adjusting business. Berliner demurred on what seemed to him the sensible ground that he knew nothing about public adjusting, a tricky line of work that involves taking inventories, being familiar with property values and assessing damage. The friend explained forcefully that a public adjuster didn't have to know anything about public adjusting: All he needed was twenty-five dollars to purchase a state license, and enough ability as a salesman to drum up trade in an overcrowded and highly competitive field. Berliner had both these qualifications; he put a manager in charge of the restaurant, went in with his friend (who knew something about public adjusting), and prospered. It wasn't long before word of Berliner's talents as a business getter reached Reilly (who knew all about public adjusting). He arranged a partnership for Berliner. Berliner's induction into the firm was only the beginning of its sudden, remarkable growth. Presently it moved from its old quarters into one of Brooklyn's newest, most stylish skyscrapers. A couple of months later it merged with another prominent outfit, Schultz, Shapiro & Goldman (Schultz was an ex-assistant fire marshal too), becoming O'Toole, McClanahan, Schultz, Goldman and Berliner, and took occupancy of an entire floor of the building. Bielaski, at that point, began feeling inquisitive about a public adjusting firm whose weekly expenses, he learned, ran close to three thousand dollars. Three thousand dollars a week, he noted, was a hundred and fifty thousand dollars a year, and to bring in a hundred and fifty thousand dollars a year, a public adjuster would have to handle at least a million and a half dollars in losses. Since the total losses in Brooklyn in 1932 were seven million dollars, (which was four million more than they should have been), Bielaski felt justified in assuming that a firm that was able to get a million and a half all by itself was using methods of salesmanship that were unusually forceful. As a matter of fact three thousand a week was too high an overhead even for a firm with forceful methods of salesmanship. O'Toole, McClanahan, Schultz, Goldman & Berliner broke up six or eight months after it was organized. Its two most spirited partners, Reilly and Berliner, thereupon set up their own firm which they forthrightly called Reilly & Berliner. Reilly & Berliner was conspicuously successful until its career was brought to an end by the breaking up of the arson ring.

That Reilly was something of an organizing genius he clearly demonstrated by the lucid account he subsequently gave in court of the legitimate side of the public adjusting business, as he conducted it for O'Toole, McClanahan, Schultz, Goldman & Berliner. He was the inside man who

stayed at his desk from early in the morning until sometimes as late as eleven at night. On that desk were two
extension telephones from the office switchboard; one instrument that answered for two private numbers of his,
and an intercommunication system with several of his partners. He spent most of his day using these telephones.
Evenings he worked on the books; he was the firm's treasurer. O'Toole, McClanahan had a branch office in Brownsville which was backed up to a fire house. On permanent
duty there from 8 A.M. to 6 P.M. was a man whose principal
job was to listen through the wall for the alarms that came
in, and to telephone them instantly to Reilly. Reilly had
obtained from the Fire Department a book listing the addresses and signals of all the alarm boxes in Brooklyn, and
he also had the Telephone Company's information direc-
tories, which list telephones by street addresses. As soon as
Brownsville called him, he looked up in the Fire Department book the box that the alarm had come from, and
then put in a call to a telephone on that block to find out
what building was burning. Frequently he was able to be
on the phone soliciting the loss by the time the engines
arrived at the fire. If the loss looked like a particularly
juicy one, he would call a partner on the intercom and
dispatch him to the fire to make a personal solicitation.

Because competition in the adjusting business had always been furious, the Public Adjusters Association, in
1925, had included in its code of fair practices, at the
insistence of the Fire Marshal, a ban on soliciting losses
between 6 P.M. and 8 A.M. To compensate the adjusters
for not allowing them to harass potential customers in the
middle of the night, the association had men on duty all
night compiling, via short wave radio from the despatch-
er's office at the Fire Department, a complete list of all

fires occurring in the proscribed period. These men, early in the morning, called representatives of all the adjusting firms and passed the list on. Reilly was the man who received the list, at his home between 6:30 and 7 A.M., for O'Toole, McClanahan. The other partners in the firm were standing by their telephones by 7:30, and Reilly called them one by one, assigning to each one the fire nearest his home. Since every alert adjusting firm followed this practice, it was an ordinary sight, at eight o'clock of a Brooklyn morning, to see a building that had been burned during the night besieged by a horde of howling adjusters who were brandishing pens and legal documents, and adjuring the unhappy victim of the flames to sign in the space designated by the x. "There were more adjusters in those days than there were fires," Bielaski recalled recently. "The smart adjusters tried to equalize the supply with the demand." As Bielaski had suspected, as Samuels' report indicated, and as later findings were to confirm, Berliner was a smart adjuster.

³ *Moe*

To Bielaski's disappointment, the third—and crucial—Sam was not nearly so easy to identify as the second. Davidoff, the soul of indiscretion about almost anything else, was strangely vague when it came to producing his mechanic. Samuels insisted that his "brother-in-law," a character who showed up from time to time in the person of another National Board operative, would have nothing to do with a fire until he had conferred directly with the man who was going to make it; Davidoff repeatedly promised to arrange such a conference, but each time he did the mysterious mechanic, at the last moment, called it off. It was only after a great deal of urging and schnapps that Davidoff late one night finally let slip that Sam the *macher's* last name was Sapphire, a revelation he regretted at once, and which did the National Board little immediate good, since no Sam Sapphire was listed in the City Directory or in the telephone book. Sapphire, it seemed, assiduously cultivated a conspiratorial atmosphere. He didn't have a telephone, but made and received calls in various phone booths strategically scattered about the more inflammable sections of the borough. Samuels was afraid to ask

Davidoff where Sapphire lived; Davidoff already felt nervous about having revealed the mechanic's name, and another direct question, Samuels was certain, would be likely to corrupt the invaluable innocence of his friend's mind. Beyond mentioning that Sapphire's wife was a very sick woman, a fact that appeared to be of small relevance to the matter at hand, Davidoff from then on was impenetrable.

Matters were resting in this unsatisfactory position when, one afternoon late in December, came the sort of break detectives frequently get if they are patient enough. Over in Manhattan, a bedraggled and furtive character who declined to identify himself by any name more elaborate than Moe, presented himself at the offices of the New York *Evening Journal* and whispered to a receptionist that he had some information of a confidential nature to convey to the publisher. He was offered an interview with a resident rewrite man, which he indignantly declined. A considerable amount of haggling ensued, the result of which was a compromise in the person of the city editor. To him Moe confided that he knew who was making the fires in Brooklyn. He hoped the city editor wouldn't misunderstand him, he went on. He genuinely regretted having been led upon the paths of evil, and he sincerely wanted to atone. But, he said, the city editor should bear in mind that helping arrange fires, although undoubtedly an anti-social way of earning a living, nevertheless was the only way he had been able to find in these lean years. He was turning upon his former associates at a considerable financial sacrifice, he said, and he had a family to support. He had read the *Evening Journal* for many years, he said, and he knew that it possessed the human touch. In brief, he said, how much was his information worth. The city editor persuaded Moe to tell his story, and discovered that it was quite unusable by any newspaper familiar with the laws of libel, although obviously of great value to a detective who wanted to inquire into the situation. Knowing that the National Board was an organization that also possessed the human touch, and that would be willing, besides, to cooperate in making such a future headline as JOURNAL HELPS SMASH ARSON RING possible, he delivered Moe over to Bielaski, imposing on the National Board only the entirely reasonable condition that any public announcements resulting from Moe's revelation should first be made in the *Evening Journal*. On the whole the city editor was rather relieved when Moe departed. Moe smoked cigars, which were always going out, and he carried loose kitchen matches in his pocket to relight them. Twenty times an hour, it seemed to the city editor, Moe would pull out a match, strike it on the sole of his shoe, hold it in the air for a moment while he looked around the room appraisingly, and then touch it to his cigar. A nasty habit, the city editor thought, a very nasty habit indeed.

Under the benign influence of the human touch, which, as he had been correctly informed, the National Board possessed, Moe held a series of edifying conferences with Bielaski. The detective was no more anxious than Moe was for the news of his defection to become public. Moe was forbidden entry to the National Board offices, so that not even the staff operatives would learn of his existence; he met Bielaski in cafeterias, subway stations, hotel lobbies and occasionally turkish baths. At all times he was voluble. The most enterprising maker of fires in Brooklyn, he said, was the public adjusting firm of Reilly & Berliner. The firm's chief mechanic was Sam Sapphire.

He knew these things because in the course of his attempts to support his wife and children (for after all if a man doesn't look out for himself, no one else will) he had thrown a certain amount of business Sapphire's way. He had expected a certain amount of gratitude in return, he added, but both Reilly & Berliner, and Sapphire, had been entirely deficient in the human touch; they had, in fact, treated him shabbily. One highly successful shoe store fire that he, Moe, had arranged by the sweat of his brow, had netted Sapphire $250, Reilly & Berliner at least $1000, and out of all that they had given Moe just twenty-five. "I thought I was dealing with honest men," Moe said. "Hitler should have for friends such honest men," he added as an ironical afterthought. Between long soliloquies in this vein, to which Bielaski listened patiently, Moe contributed a number of details to the National Board's dossier on Sapphire. He gave an accurate and detailed personal description of Sapphire. He revealed that Sapphire lived in a two-family house on Dahill Road in the vicinity of the Bensonhurst end of King's Highway. He said that Sapphire had a method of setting fires all his own, the secret of which he guarded jealously, but that it involved carrying to the scene of the crime, in a shabby, blue 1929 Essex, a large parcel done up in brown paper. He said that Sapphire was a highly talented ladies' man, and the fact that he had a wife who was seriously ill seemed rather to increase than to curtail his activities in that direction. Moe expressed himself as perfectly willing to point Sapphire out to a National Board detective any time he was asked to, but Bielaski decided not to let Moe expose himself even to that limited extent unless it proved absolutely necessary. He felt that with the information about Sapphire he now possessed, he could

18141

easily be found by orthodox methods. Moe he was saving for bigger things; he wanted him to improve his acquaintance with Sapphire to a point from which he would be able to notify the National Board of the precise time and place of an impending fire, thus enabling the authorities to apprehend the mechanic just as he was touching a match to the contents of one of his brown paper parcels. On the grounds that a man had to look out for his own skin, because no one else would, Moe at first expressed some repugnance for this program, but a liberal application of the human touch overcame his scruples.

When Bielaski had dredged out of Moe everything he could about Sapphire's history, personality and habits he passed on the information to Samuels on Mansfield Place; Samuels received them, like a good soldier, without questioning their source. Dahill Road was close to his home— as opposed to his temporary bachelor quarters on Mansfield Place—and so he set the invaluable Mrs. Samuels to watching Sapphire's house. There were several men in the house who looked pretty much alike, though, and she couldn't be sure which was Sapphire. Then, one morning, toward the middle of January, she observed one of the men park a shabby blue 1929 Essex near the intersection of McDonald Avenue and Quentin Road, a busy corner not far from the house, and enter a stationery store there. She followed him in. The man was in affectionate conversation with the pretty proprietress of the store; she, apparently, was cashing a check for him, and she was smiling coyly at his jocular compliments. After one particularly pointed tribute to her charms, she said, "Your poor sick wife, how is she?"

"She should drop dead, sugar," the man said gaily.

The girl screwed her face into an unconvincing expression of disapproval, said, "Tchk, tchk, tchk," and beamed. The man pinched her cheek, left the store, climbed into the Essex and drove away.

"I know that fellow from somewheres, I swear," Mrs. Samuels said. "What's his name?"

"He's a big dress manufacturer lives on Dahill Road," said the storekeeper. "Mr. Sapphire."

"I'd like some of those cute paper doilies for a mahjongg party," said Mrs. Samuels. "Three dozen if you got them."

Four days later, the pretty storekeeper was informed by her bank that a $35 check signed by Samuel Sapphire, which she had deposited to her account, had bounced.

It took several days to devise a sufficiently circumspect scheme for pointing out Sapphire to the National Board staff. During that time his wife died, a circumstance that caused Mrs. Samuels acute private discomfort. Sapphire, in accordance with religious custom, confined himself to his house for a seven-day period of mourning. On the fifth day Mrs. Samuels presented herself at the door as a vender of tickets to a Hadassah benefit, and asked for Mrs. Sapphire. She expressed shock at being informed by Sapphire of Mrs. Sapphire's decease, and begged to be excused for intruding on his grief. Not at all, he said, and invited her in. She reluctantly complied and explained to him that some weeks before Mrs. Sapphire had purchased two tickets to the benefit, but that she had not paid for them. Sapphire paid her, and courteously ushered her back to the front hall. His dog, a small, off-white mongrel, accompanied them there. As Sapphire opened the front door, Mrs. Samuels managed to give the dog a surreptitious kick that sent it howling into the street. Sapphire rushed out in pursuit. A National Board operative, sitting in a parked car, made a minute scrutiny of Sapphire's face and figure as he recovered the pet, and then drove off contentedly. It was, perhaps, a bizarre way of putting the finger on a man, but detectives, like all skilled workmen, like to give a job an artistic fillip now and then. The three dollars that Sapphire had paid for the non-existent tickets, were conceded by all hands to be the rightful property of Mrs. Samuels as an incidental emolument that she richly deserved. It more than covered the cost of the doilies.

4 *Sam the* Macher

At the time of Mrs. Samuels' call, Sam Sapphire might well have been taken for a moderately prosperous and thoroughly undistinguished small businessman. He was short and sturdily built. He had a high forehead, curly black hair and brown eyes whose expression was effectively masked by thick-lensed spectacles. He dressed neatly and conservatively; he seldom used profanity or liquor; despite his nonchalant attitude toward his invalid wife, he was devoted to his four sons, who ranged in age from six to twenty-one. His manner of speaking, which was confidential, wordy and just a shade importunate, was precisely that of a hard-working shopkeeper whose life had been honorably dedicated to maintaining that muskrat was mink or to selling size 5AAA shoes to ladies with size 7C feet. This bland exterior, however, concealed a turbulent soul. Sapphire in his own eyes was not an inoffensive little man with modest attainments, but a hero whose true worth had remained unrecognized because of the incredible obtuseness—or the shameful corruption—of the world. This delusion made his life a good deal more complex than the average man's—or perhaps even than the average hero's. In addition to being a highly skilled incendiary, he had, through the years, been charged with or suspected of forgery, embezzlement, burglary and reckless driving; he was an experienced writer of phony checks, and just one week after his wife died, in circumstances that most quarters would consider tragic, he gaily set up housekeeping with the undivorced mother of a thirteen-year-old daughter. Among his friends he was considered a man of unusual charm.

Because Sapphire could bring himself to tell the truth only when he had a compelling motive to do so—such a motive, say, as making sure, once he was caught, that all his fellow conspirators would be caught too—the details of his biography are obscure. He was certainly born in Russia, but whether it was in Ukraine or in White Russia, in 1884 or in 1889, seem to have been matters for considerable disagreement between Sapphire and himself. The family came to Millville, New Jersey, when Sam was in his teens, and a few years later moved to the Lower East Side of New York. Not much more time passed before Sapphire had become a familiar traveler on the paths of unrighteousness. It appears likely, for one thing, that an early involvement of his was with a fleet of taxicabs whose revenue derived largely from carrying immigrants from the docks on the West Side to their relatives on the East Side at ten dollars a head. Special treatment was reserved for passengers who appeared knowing enough to question such a large price for such a small ride: They were taken from the West Side to the East Side by way of the Brooklyn Bridge, and charged twenty-five dollars. At other times in the period before the first war, Sapphire was apparently connected with various Rivington Street establishments that dealt in one or other of the two basic varieties of apparel—stolen and not stolen. His first documented appearance in the world was in Detroit in 1919 and 1920. There he bought a small dressmaking business from an acquaintance for $660. Before he got around to making the first payment, the business failed. The acquaintance, who must have been an exceptionally good-natured man, took the insolvent Sapphire into his home to live. Sapphire stayed two or three months and then, one night when his host and hostess were out, disappeared. A diamond bracelet belonging to the hostess disappeared at the very same time, but the Detroit police were never able to prove that this was more than an amusing coincidence. Sapphire, in later years, always maintained that the husband himself had done away with the bracelet in order to collect the insurance on it, an explanation which, whether true or false, was quite consistent with the environment in which Sapphire habitually moved.

A year later Sapphire was visible in New York again as the proprietor of a knitgoods factory from which, for a while, he seems to have made a substantial—and honest—living. In 1922, however, the bottom fell out of the Japanese silk market, in which he had invested heavily, and he found himself with more than $100,000 in debts. It seemed evident to him that the only sensible course of action under the circumstances was to have a fire in the factory, which was insured for seventy-nine thousand dollars. Through a well-connected rag-buyer of his acquaintance he was introduced to a Jersey City "torch"—as professional incendiaries are often called and call themselves—who offered to set the fire for five thousand dollars. Sapphire haggled with the man until he had beaten the price down to four thousand, and then gave him a two hundred dollar deposit and told him to go ahead. The fire occurred as agreed, but all Sapphire was able to extract from his insurance company was $46,000, even after he had conscientiously seared all his knitting machines with a blow torch, and then poured water over them, to simulate the damage that should have been caused by the fire and fireman but hadn't. He was able to pick up a few thousand more, after the insurance company's check came, by having one of his employees rub down the machines with kerosene, which removed the rust and enabled him to sell them as like new. There is no particular reason to believe that he paid the torch the $3800 he owed him.

The years between 1922 and 1931 Sapphire spent drifting in and out of dress businesses, cleaning and dyeing businesses, fur businesses: whatever businesses seemed to show promise of making him a dollar. Few of them fulfilled their promise, however, and he became addicted to passing worthless checks. Now and then he tried his hand at forgery, an art for which he never displayed much talent, but at which he managed to do better than he deserved. Early in 1929 he walked into the branch of the Chase National Bank in the Metropolitan Life Insurance Company building and cashed a fifteen hundred dollar check signed with the name of one of the bank's depositors. It wasn't very many hours later that the bank discovered the check was a forgery, and a pretty crude one at that. The next day he returned to the bank with another check signed with another depositor's name. Before he had even presented it, he was arrested and charged with second degree forgery. He retained the venerable criminal lawyer James D. C. Murray as his counsel. Murray consulted a handwriting expert, who, after charging Sapphire $40 for his services, declared flatly that Sapphire had indeed forged the two checks. Murray promptly advised Sapphire that he would undoubtedly be convicted, and that he should, therefore, plead guilty to a lesser count. Sapphire thanked him for the advice, and followed it. A few weeks later he was sentenced to two years in jail. When he heard the sentence he leaped up screaming that he was innocent, and that he had only pleaded guilty for expediency. He was carted off to the Tombs, still yelling, but from that vantage point he presently induced Murray to go back to the judge and ask to have the plea changed. The judge agreed, and Sapphire was let out on bail. The trial was not held until April, 1933, at which time jurymen didn't have much sympathy for banks. Sapphire was acquitted. Meanwhile, the $40 check Sapphire had given the handwriting expert had bounced.

Ever since his Rivington Street days Sapphire had been familiar with the axiom that the best way to keep a business out of bankruptcy was to burn it down. Being an observant, easily educable fellow, he had also acquired a number of useful pointers on the technique of fire-making from the same school. On one occasion a man who operated a shoe store on Rivington Street had burned his place. It was a bungled job. He had used gasoline, and the policeman on the beat had smelled it, so it became necessary to persuade the policeman not to report the evidence of his senses to his superiors. The storekeeper felt that if he personally handed the policeman the seventy-five dollars (the price, apparently, was standard, in conformity with a sort of unofficial fair trade practices act) it might be construed as bribery, so he asked Sapphire to deliver the money. The policeman, after pocketing the bills, expressed his contempt toward a man so ignorant as to use gasoline. Celluloid was the thing, he told Sapphire. It made no smoke, left no ash and produced a flash fire that would neatly destroy the entire contents of a store without endangering the occupants of the building, and that would die down by the time the engines arrived. Sapphire never forgot these words, whose wisdom was borne out by the Jersey City torch who burned the knit-goods factory. He used celluloid, and produced a fire that no one for a moment suspected was incendiary.

A man who played an even more inspirational part in Sapphire's incendiary career than the Rivington Street policeman was a friend named Maurice Jaffe. Jaffe was a man fifteen or twenty years older than Sapphire who was an extremely successful public adjuster. Specializing in Lower East Side trade, Jaffe, whose offices were in John Street, in the heart of the insurance district, was one of the most active and best-loved men in the business. When he died, in 1931, his funeral procession was convoyed, fore and aft, by motorcycle policemen, and contained several carfuls of police inspectors, fire chiefs and district leaders. One reason Jaffe was successful was that when business was slow he did not hesitate to stimulate it by having a judicious fire or two made to order. It was Jaffe, a kindly man who valued his friends, who suggested to Sapphire that he could pick up some extra cash, when he needed it, making fires, and who, thereafter, threw as many fires as he could Sapphire's way. It was Jaffe, also, who introduced Sapphire to that indispensable part of any mechanic's equipment, the plumber's tallow candle, which when lit and placed in proximity to the accelerant (as celluloid or gasoline are termed in criminological circles) serves as a time fuse. Sapphire had the instincts of a craftsman, and he experimented tirelessly with candles until he was able, by adjusting their length, to time the outbreak of his fires almost to the minute. By 1930 he had not made many fires—three or four for needy relatives and ten or fifteen for Jaffe—but he had thoroughly learned how to make them.

Early in 1931 Sapphire and a friend named Sol Cohen, who couldn't read or write (he could add and subtract, though), opened a shabby dress store in downtown Brooklyn which they called the Wonder Apparel Shop. It did about as well as a business that was founded in 1931 might have been expected to do. At the end of five weeks, Sapphire was happy to sell his share to Cohen for five hundred dollars, taking two hundred and fifty in cash and Cohen's note for the remainder. Cohen made no effort to pay off the note, however, and Sapphire, after waiting around for a couple of months, became irritated. "Sol," he said to his erstwhile partner, "I'm going to get that money if I have to burn the place down,"—which, on June 27, was exactly what he did. Although Cohen had not been consulted about the fire, there is no evidence that it made him miserable. He placed his insurance claim in the hands of Reilly, who was then working for O'Toole, McClanahan and Co. Insurance settlements have a way of dragging along. By September Sapphire still hadn't been paid his two hundred and fifty dollars, so he called on Reilly to find out if matters couldn't be expedited. Reilly put him in touch with a Mr. Winograd, a nearby clothing merchant who carried on a profitable sideline of buying up fire claims, before they were paid, at a twenty-five percent discount, and of lending money with unpaid losses as collateral—a perfectly legal business even if it doesn't sound like it. He agreed to lend Cohen $1000 on the Wonder Apparel Shop claim. Arranging the details of this transaction involved a number of conferences between Cohen and members of the adjusting firm. At one of these sessions Cohen blurted out that the Wonder Apparel Shop fire had been an act of Sapphire, not God. This, presumably, was delightful news to the adjuster who heard it. Sapphire was summoned to the O'Toole, McClanahan offices in downtown Brooklyn where, in October, a working arrangement between the firm and Sapphire was suggested, whereby the firm would give Sapphire any prospective fires it obtained, and Sapphire would give O'Toole, McClanahan the adjustment of the losses from fires he scared up for himself. This was the beginning of Sapphire's career as a full-time arsonist. It was also the beginning of a lustrous, if brief, era in the affairs of O'Toole, McClanahan & Co. It should be noted that, at his subsequent trial for arson, Reilly denied flatly that he had ever been party to any such agreement with Sapphire, or had, in fact, transacted any business of an incendiary nature. The jury convicted him of having done so, but the verdict was set aside by an appellate court, and upon being tried a second time he was acquitted.

The hundred or so fires that Sapphire made in his nineteen months of full-time activity were not all in Brooklyn. His reputation as a good workman spread rapidly, and before long he was in demand as far away as Bergen County, New Jersey. A good part of his work came from Maurice Jaffe & Co. Maurice Jaffe had died, but he was succeeded in the business by his twenty-two-year-old son, Irving, who had learned the trade at his father's knee, and whom Sapphire had known as a child. Irving, if anything, was more sentimental than his father, and gladly gave his dear old friend a number of Manhattan fires. When he didn't have any fires ready to hand, he went to extraordinary lengths to create situations in which fires would be called for. One interesting project he cooked up required

Sapphire to rent an apartment on East Second Street under the name of Mr. Harry Rosencrantz, and to fill it with furniture picked up at junk shops for a total outlay of, perhaps, fifty dollars. He insured the furniture for $2500 with an insurance broker named Horowitz. After waiting a couple of months for the policy to become ripe and juicy, he made a fire, and gave the insurance claim to Jaffe to adjust. Jaffe figured he could get about $1800 for the loss, which was to be split, in equal shares, among Sapphire, Horowitz and himself. Unfortunately, just as the claim was put in, the insurance company fell into financial difficulties, so Jaffe hastily settled for $775. When the company failed to collapse, a few months later, Sapphire felt very badly used. What with one thing of this sort and another, Sapphire averaged $150 or $200 a week, a handsome income in those days even for a skilled mechanic.

No income short of Louis B. Mayer's would have been handsome enough for Sapphire, though. He had always been a big spender, a give-the-man-five-dollars-for-his-trouble boy, and now, being an intrepid arsonist, he had a position to live up to besides. When he bought a five cent cup of coffee in a lunchroom, he left a quarter on the counter for the waitress; when he bought a shirt—which was seldom, since he made numerous fires for impoverished haberdashers—he disdained to pay less than ten dollars; when he craved female companionship, which was constantly, no investment of cash seemed to him too large. The habitual debility of his finances was partly caused, also, by the complex business procedures indigenous to the manufacture, distribution and sale of fires. Every time Sapphire made a fire without receiving full payment in advance he took the chance of not getting paid at all, since the business ethics of the people he dealt with were in no way more chaste than his own, and it would have been difficult for him to have gone to law over non-payment. But if he had refused to make fires without being paid in advance, he would have been unemployed, since most of his clients were eager for fires precisely because they had no cash on hand. This dilemma forced him to accept obviously worthless IOUs from his clients, and to trust the public adjusters with whom he was dealing to see that the notes were made good when the insurance company checks came through. (Public adjusters always got paid for *their* services, because the checks came through them.) Even assuming that such fellows as Berliner were trustworthy, which is quite an assumption, Sapphire still, more often than not, had difficulty collecting, because a client's legitimate creditors had generally established claims to two or three hundred percent of the insurance check before it had even been written, or else, to elude these creditors, the client had sold the loss to the obliging Mr. Winograd, and the twenty-five percent discount Mr. Winograd had exacted included the money that was to have gone to Sapphire. Sapphire found himself spending more working hours perpetrating elaborate financial deals, such as selling IOUs back to the signers at substantial discounts, and attempting to blackmail extra cash from his clients with threats to tell all to the police, than he did selling or manufacturing fires. He continued to pass rubber checks and to refuse to pay his bills. At the time of his arrest he had $1200 outstanding in uncollected fees.

5 *Sapphire observed*

None of the foregoing details of Sapphire's career, of course, was known to Bielaski at the time the *macher's* name first came up. All Bielaski knew was that after expending three months, several thousand dollars and incalculable ingenuity, he had finally discovered the identity of a man who was supposed to be an arsonist. He still had to prove it, a troublesome task at best, since the act of deliberately setting a fire is one designed to destroy most of the evidence that the fire was deliberately set. Sapphire was immediately put under rigorous observation—or, more accurately, an attempt was made to put Sapphire under rigorous observation, for it turned out that keeping an eye on Sapphire, a job that would theoretically be elementary for a corps of trained sleuths, was actually embarrassingly complicated. Sapphire seldom ventured forth without the blue Essex, and once he was behind its wheel, his eyes peered through his thick lenses with a malignant glare, and he became as a man possessed. Speed limits and parking regulations he overlooked habitually and as a matter of principle; one-way street signs, if he was in a mellow mood, he occasionally heeded, but he refused to take any notice at all of traffic lights. His astounded pursuers first tried to keep up with him when he went for a ride, but after suffering a number of humiliating interviews with traffic policemen, during which the blue Essex would disappear over the horizon, careening crazily, they decided that the only way they could make sure of not losing him was to use a car with a siren. This seemed just a bit impractical for men who wanted to keep their activities unnoticed. Scarcely a week passed, of course, during which Sapphire didn't get a traffic summons or two. He never answered them, but merely turned them over to Berliner to fix, which that gentleman, as head of the Borough Hall Boys, always promised to do and never did. Nevertheless, Sapphire, perhaps because he changed his address frequently, was never brought to book for his driving. In 1936, at which time he was languishing in Clinton Prison, a newspaper reporter, rummaging through some records in Brooklyn Police Headquarters, came upon a warrant that had been issued against Sapphire a couple of months previously for failing to answer 72 vintage traffic tickets. Across the warrant was scrawled, "Cannot be located."

Shortly after the death of his wife Sapphire left Dahill Road and moved in and out of a series of rooming houses and hotels, accompanied by his three youngest sons and a small peroxide blonde named Mrs. Sarah Gordon. Baby, as Sapphire called Mrs. Gordon, had been his principal girl friend for years; neither saw much point in concealing the fact any longer. She took care of Sapphire's children, drove around with him in the blue Essex, and made herself useful in a number of ways. Her husband, a storekeeper near Chatham Square in Manhattan, refused to give her a divorce. For a few days Sapphire and Baby had a room at the Hotel St. George. While they were there Bielaski kept a man firmly planted in a lobby armchair to check on their comings and goings. One afternoon, when they came into the lobby, Sapphire looked around warily, caught sight of the detective, who immediately became fascinated by the recipes in the *Sun,* and scrutinized him for several moments before going up in the elevator. The detective became uneasy but decided to remain at his post. Fifteen minutes later Sapphire came into the lobby and walked up to the detective, who was still enthusiastically studying recipes. "You're a detective," he announced flatly. The detective heatedly denied it, but Sapphire was unperturbed. "Never mind the hooey," he said. "Just tell that heel Gordon he's not needing detectives. Tell him he should come himself and she'll give him all the evidence he wants." He went back upstairs.

At the beginning of April Sapphire and Baby abandoned their nomad existence and settled down, under the name of Mr. & Mrs. Gordon, in an apartment in the Hotel Lafayette in downtown Brooklyn. It was an imprudent thing to do, since it enabled Bielaski's men to tap Sapphire's telephone and to at last establish the kind of watch on him that daredevil driving was powerless to frustrate. Those were the days when tapping telephones was unrestricted, and Bielaski showed that his ethics were of a high grade by securing the approval of the Brooklyn District Attorney, William Francis Xavier Geoghan, before cutting in on Sapphire's line. Ever since Sapphire had been identified, the National Board had kept Geoghan informed of the progress of the investigation, and Geoghan had promised to cooperate in any way he could.

Sapphire's conversations for the first few days provided little direct evidence of his activities, but they at least revealed with whom he was associating. April 13, the day he was acquitted of forgery, was the day the wire was tapped. Sapphire's first call that afternoon was to Irving Jaffe, the son and successor in the adjusting business of Sapphire's late friend Maurice. He told Irving about the verdict and received his congratulations. A few minutes later a Dr. Hess called him and asked him when he was going to pay the bill he owed. Sapphire said he'd be around the next day. The doctor asked how Baby was feeling; Sapphire said she was feeling better, and the doctor said he was sure she'd be all right. (A check on Dr. Hess by Bielaski disclosed that he had been involved in an unexplained fire, adjusted by Reilly & Berliner, the year before.) Sapphire then called his laundry and demanded that his clothes be delivered. The girl at the laundry said they would be if he'd only pay his bill. Sapphire said to send the driver around the next afternoon. The driver came the next afternoon and called Sapphire from the lobby. Sapphire asked how much he owed. The driver said $9.80. "$9.80?" Sapphire said. "The hell with you. I can buy new stuff." (This episode was repeated at least three times during the month that Sapphire's phone was tapped, and apparently, toward the end of this time, Sapphire was quite desperately trying to find a men's clothing store that needed burning.) Dr. Hess called again immediately after the driver left. Sapphire apologized profusely for not having come around; he'd been in an automobile accident, he said. This was an out-and-out lie, but the doctor was apparently familiar with Sapphire's driving technique and believed every word of it. Hess never did get his money, nor did the telephone company, nor did a number of individuals who had made Sapphire personal loans, nor did the Lafayette Hotel. One day the hotel manager called to ask when the hotel bill was going to be paid. "Believe me, Mr. McCabe, this thing is making me sick," Sapphire told him. "Believe me, Mr. Gordon, it's making me sick too," Mr. McCabe answered, and hung up.

Diverting as all this was to Bielaski, when he read the reports, it provided very little evidence that Sapphire was an arsonist. Then, toward the end of April Bielaski received encouraging word from Moe, who had succeeded in maintaining friendly relations with Sapphire. Moe reported that Sapphire had met a certain Monroe Moscowitz, a shoe manufacturer and jobber, an acquaintance of Moe's. Moscowitz, it seemed, thought that maybe he wanted a fire in his factory, but he wasn't sure. Because the factory job would be a $500 affair, Sapphire had agreed to make a trial run in the form of a small fire in Moscowitz's apartment, for the bargain rate of $50. If the apartment fire proved a success, Moe said, the factory fire would follow. Moe's story was confirmed by Sapphire's telephone conversations, a good many of which were with Moscowitz. Mostly they concerned money, and there was a good deal of chaffering over whether a certain five dollars that Moscowitz had presumably loaned Sapphire would be deducted from the $50, as Moscowitz maintained, or whether the original price had been $55, which meant the five had already been deducted, as Sapphire insisted. Several times it looked as if the deal would be called off over the five dollars, and once it almost fell through because Sapphire and Moscowitz couldn't agree on a place to meet to discuss arrangements. Moscowitz favored the corner of Fulton Street and Myrtle Avenue, which Sapphire regarded as insecure, and he held out for the area near the change booth in the DeKalb Avenue BMT station. Finally, to the intense relief of Bielaski, who had waited for months for this kind of opportunity, they agreed on the swimming pool of the Hotel St. George. This bickering took a couple of weeks which, actually, was a remarkably short time for a fire to be arranged in.

On May 13 the listeners intercepted a call from Baby to a button factory in Long Island City. She asked for a Mr. Ford, and told him to prepare a bundle of scrap celluloid for Mr. Wall who would call for it that afternoon. Mr. Ford, who apparently was familiar with Mr. Wall's requirements, said he would be glad to. Bielaski found this call particularly helpful. He had been fairly certain for some months that Sapphire's fire-making technique involved celluloid, since most of the suspicious fires that he believed him to have made had been distinguished by an absence of smoke and ash. A few months before, furthermore, an attempted fire in a shoe factory had failed because the incendiary had placed his celluloid directly under the factory's sprinkler system, which, of course, had extinguished the blaze as soon as it had started. It had been a mistake a nearsighted man could easily have made. The afternoon of Baby's phone call a detective managed to stay on the blue Essex's trail long enough to see Sapphire to the button factory, and to watch him emerge a few minutes later carrying a large cardboard box which he put in the back seat of the car. May 14 was a Sunday; Bielaski stood by anxiously, awaiting word about the time and place of the Moscowitz job, but no word came through. The next day, though, Sapphire called Moscowitz and made a final appointment with him for 8:30 A.M. on the 17th, at Moscowitz's apartment on Ocean Avenue. Delighted at the prospect of some direct action after six months of enforced guile, Bielaski immediately informed Geoghan and Fire Marshal Thomas Patrick

Brophy, with whose office he always worked closely, that the time had come to arrest Brooklyn's most proficient fire maker in the very act of making a fire. They also informed the city editor of the *Evening Journal*. On the morning of the 17th the block on which Moscowitz lived was jammed with police detectives, assistant fire marshals, and agents in the employ of the National Board. At 8:55 (Sapphire, for all his haste, never got anywhere on time) the blue Essex pulled up in front of the apartment house. Sapphire climbed out, retrieved the cardboard box from the back seat, and entered the building. Brophy, a police inspector, and sundry aides, followed him in, after making sure that he was in Moscowitz's ground floor apartment. Twenty minutes later Sapphire and Moscowitz, both looking flustered, emerged, without the cardboard box. Brophy stepped forward and laid a large hand on the shoulder of each of them. Meanwhile a squad of officials burst into Moscowitz's apartment to douse the lighted candle they expected to find there. To their chagrin there was no lighted candle. The cardboard box, its contents intact, was reposing on a shelf in the bedroom closet. It was too late by then to call off the arrest and start all over again. Brophy turned the men over to the police, who carted them off to a handy precinct, booked them and began a course of interrogation that, as far as Sapphire was concerned was to last, under various auspices, for several years.

6 *A trip to Staten Island*

While Sapphire had been enjoying his last weeks at large,
Sam Samuels, the inside man, had been furiously accumulating evidence that would refute Sapphire if he denied
everything, or corroborate him if he admitted all. He had
managed for all those months to keep Abe Davidoff convinced that the hat factory on Seventeenth Street needed
burning, while continuing to demur to the fire on the
grounds that Sam the *macher* didn't appear to be trustworthy. Davidoff regarded Mrs. Rose Bernstein, the lady
whom Samuels mentioned in a previous report as having
had her ice cream parlor burned by Sapphire, as his most
contented customer. He was determined to bring Mrs.
Bernstein and Samuels together, but he didn't know Mrs.
Bernstein's address and it took him months to find it. Finally Samuels was able to report:

"On May 4th, 1933, your Agent picked up Abe Davidoff
at his home at 8:00 a.m. as per arrangement and proceeded
by way of 39th Street Ferry to St. George, Staten Island.
Davidoff had the address of Mrs. Bernstein. While
Davidoff made inquiries there, your Agent got in conversation in a drug store across the street with one S——. He

asked me what I was doing around there and I mentioned the name of Bernstein, whereupon S—— led me into Bernstein's place, which is a fruit and vegetable store operated by Joe Bernstein. Joe Bernstein is the husband of Mrs. Bernstein. In the short conversation I had with Joe Bernstein I said: 'You look familiar to me.' He replied: 'Oh, I used to live in Brooklyn—I had an ice cream parlor on 13th Avenue.' I asked him: 'What did you do with the place, sell it?' His answer was: 'Oh no, my wife had the place burned.' I asked him: 'How do you know, "vas you there, Sharley?"' whereupon Bernstein answered: 'Oh, I know all right, she told me so the day after the fire, that woman is capable of doing anything.' By that time Davidoff had returned and was greeted very friendly by both S—— and Joe Bernstein. Bernstein then, in the presence of Davidoff, told me that the job, meaning the fire, was not a profitable one and they did not get anything for themselves out of the insurance as it was immediately attached by a number of creditors and they would have been better off if they did not have the place burned. Davidoff said: 'If I would have known your financial difficulties I would have advised you differently.' Bernstein then told your Agent and Davidoff that he has not been living with his wife for several months; that she resides alone with their youngest daughter, a girl about 16 years of age, at the Ambassador Apartment, St. George, a little ways up the hill from the fruit store; that his wife has a sweetheart, Morris C——, also known as Mersha; that this Morris C—— supports her. Your Agent and Davidoff then proceeded to the Ambassador Apartments. When I entered the apartment Davidoff took me by my arm and introduced me to Mrs. Bernstein, saying: 'This is Sam, one of my very best friends.' After shaking hands with Mrs.

Bernstein, I remarked: 'Don't confuse me with the other
Sam,' whereupon she replied: 'Oh, I know you are not the
other Sam, I know him very well.' She served drinks (liquor) and also served some refreshments for Davidoff who,
as usual, was hungry. The conversation drifted to the
death of Sam Sapphire's wife, whereupon I spoke up and
said: 'Who care anything about them people,' and, turning to Mrs. Bernstein, I said: 'All I want to know is how
good a mechanic Sam is.' Her quick answer was: 'One of
the best as far as I know. He sure did a complete job for
me.' Davidoff kept on nudging me and passed the remark
not to speak so much, but I disregarded his efforts to silence me. Mrs. Bernstein said that she was going to New
York to see her dentist. She got dressed and the three of
us left the apartment. We entered my coupe which was
parked in front of the apartment house. I drove down hill
and stopped a block away from S——'s tailor shop as
Davidoff wanted to say good bye to S——. While Davidoff
was away I asked Mrs. Bernstein what Sam used to set the
fire. Her answer was: 'He used something I don't know
what it would be called but it looked like ribbon, the kind
they trim windows of stationery and cigar stores with as it
came off a big roll. He placed it under the counter and
fixtures.' I asked her: 'When did he do it?' and she said:
'On the evening of the fire. He came in about eleven
o'clock and worked on it while I was in the store.' I asked
her: 'Who else was in the store?' She said: 'No one else
but myself.' I asked her: 'Where was your husband?' and
she said: 'I sent the lummox away.' I said: 'Where to?'
and her answer was that Mr. C—— her sweetheart, drove
him to Atlantic City Friday afternoon, the day before the
fire and returned Saturday afternoon after the fire. She
said: 'Sam (meaning Sapphire) told me that the fire

would come off four o'clock in the morning and, believe me, it did happen just to the second.' I asked her: 'How did you know, did you live upstairs over the store?' She said: 'No, I lived two blocks away and I did not sleep a wink that night and four o'clock I heard a terrific explosion and I knew it was my store.' By this time Davidoff returned to the car and we proceeded to the Whitehall Street Ferry, got aboard the ferry and on the way over Mrs. Bernstein spoke of starting a little business, sort of a private speakeasy, either at her home where she resides at present or she would move to Brooklyn, also to have one or two girls to entertain tired businessmen. Before parting with Mrs. Bernstein she asked me to call her up any time I desired and she would be glad to meet me and come out any time I wished her to."

Appended to this epic were brief descriptions of Mr. and Mrs. Bernstein and of Mrs. Bernstein's sweetheart, C——. Mrs. Bernstein was described as "about 38 to 40; light complexion; about 5′6″; weighs about 165 to 170 pounds; rather attractive looking; light henna hair; uses plenty of rouge and lipstick; dresses smartly." Poor Joe Bernstein, apparently, was "a man about 38 to 40; smooth shaven; 5′ 7″; weighs about 150 pounds; dark complexion; dark hair; wears tortoise shell glasses with metal temples; big wide open eyes; speaks with a smile." Mrs. Bernstein's sweetheart, Samuels discovered, had an invalid wife and five children. In the next few days Samuels met Mrs. Bernstein twice more, both times without Davidoff. The first time she volunteered to personally tell Samuel's mythical brother-in-law what a good mechanic Sapphire was. The following day Samuels produced the agent who was impersonating his brother-in-law, and Mrs. Bernstein did tell him. She even offered to get in touch with Sapphire then and there (on the understanding she would get ten percent of the fee for the hat factory job) but the brother-in-law agent said he didn't want to be rushed.

This last conversation, held at lunch in Child's Restaurant on Sixth Avenue and Seventeenth Street, took place only six days before Sapphire's arrest. As soon as that arrest was made, detectives were sent about the city to pick up all implicated parties. Mrs. Bernstein was, of course, one of the first to be tapped. A couple of men were also despatched to bring in Davidoff. To the National Board's embarrassment Davidoff was nowhere to be found. He had left town three days before, while Samuels had been immersed in preparations for Sapphire's arrest. There was no implication that he had known what was coming and had flown the coop; apparently he had simply decided that he couldn't make a living in New York, and had decided to try his luck elsewhere. Davidoff's son was not eager to divulge his father's whereabouts.

7 *Sam converses*

During the first few hours of his confinement, Moscowitz, a melancholy wisp of a man with a mottled complexion that led some of his more jocular acquaintances to call him Al Capone, was entirely uncommunicative, aside from repeated protestations of innocence. Sapphire, on the other hand, proved to be a nimble conversationalist; his questioners would have been captivated by the effortless flow of his speech if they had only been able to overcome the uneasy feeling that he was not being altogether candid with them. He asserted that he and Moscowitz had been engaged in a perfectly legitimate transaction over shoes. He disclaimed all knowledge of the contents of the cardboard box, stating that a mutual friend had given it to him to deliver to Moscowitz and that he had carried out the errand in good faith. When he had been searched after the arrest a stump of tallow candle had been found in his coat pocket. Sapphire accounted for its presence on his person by relating an elaborate and rather entertaining story about the day a fuse blew out in the basement of the house where his oldest son lived, and how he descended into the darkness with this candle, which he

had found in the kitchen, repaired the fuse and then carelessly pocketed the candle. When asked what he worked at
to make a living, he said, in a dignified way, "I don't
work," and let it go at that. Late in the afternoon Mrs.
Bernstein was ushered in. District Attorney Geoghan
questioned her himself. For an hour or two she flatly
refused to commit herself. Geoghan finally was forced
to agree not to prosecute her if she talked, a promise that
immediately dissolved her reticence. She told much the
same story that she had told Samuels. She said she had
paid Sapphire the $300—which she had had to raise by
signing a still unliquidated note at a bank—on the sidewalk in front of the store, in Davidoff's presence, and that
Sapphire had then and there given Davidoff the $50 he
was entitled to for introducing him to her. Later that evening Mr. Ford of the button works was brought in. He
identified Sapphire as the man who, in the guise of a toy
manufacturer named Wall, bought scrap celluloid from
him frequently, including the preceding Saturday. Moscowitz was brought back and confronted with some of this
evidence. He condescended to admit that he and Sapphire
had had a small plot on foot, but it was just "to make a
little smoke; the word fire was never mentioned between
us." He said that he had given Sapphire $35 (which the
detectives had found on him that morning,) but that Sapphire had refused to make even smoke until he got the
other $10—apparently the five dollar dispute had been
settled Moscowitz's way—and that the two of them were
on their way to Moscowitz's office to get the other ten
when they were arrested. Baby was summoned and she
sensibly admitted that she had indeed called Mr. Ford at
the button works to make the appointment for Mr. Wall.
When Sapphire, after midnight, was apprised of the testi-

mony of Mrs. Bernstein, Mr. Ford, Moscowitz, Baby, and the wire tappers, he agreed that his previous statement about not working had been, perhaps, evasive, and he brusquely admitted the nature of his profession. He confirmed Moscowitz's story about the ten dollars, but he declared that he never had any intention of burning Moscowitz's apartment, because he didn't believe the shoe factory deal would ever go through. He had originally consented to do business with Al Capone, he said, out of friendship for the man who introduced them—presumably Moe—but as he got to know Moscowitz better he came to trust him less, and he had finally resolved that the wisest course for him was to take the fifty dollars and not do the job.

Aside from admitting he had plotted with Moscowitz, and that he had made the Bernstein fire—which he couldn't very well deny in the face of Mrs. Bernstein's extremely circumstantial testimony—Sapphire kept his mouth shut for six or seven weeks, during which time he languished in the Raymond Street Jail in default of $50,-000 bail. Apparently he was awaiting word from his influential friends at Reilly & Berliner. It wasn't until the first week in July that he became persuaded that no one at Reilly & Berliner had any intention of getting him out, and he vengefully resolved to get them in. He announced he was ready to talk. His story started, "There was once a firm called Reilly & Berliner, they should drop dead," and went on from there. He admitted in specific detail to fifty-four fires in Brooklyn and numerous others in other boroughs; he implied his involvement in a hundred more. The last one he made, he said triumphantly, had been a very successful one in a beauty parlor, just four days before his arrest; a National Board agent blushed quietly as he remembered his frustration on the night of the 13th, when Sapphire drove through six red lights on Eastern Parkway and lost him. Once Sapphire started to talk in earnest his bail was reduced to $16,000, which the National Board provided. Bielaski put him on a forty-dollar-a-week salary, and he began to devote himself wholeheartedly to his new employers.

Sapphire had made so many fires for so many different people, and he had conspired with so many more people in connection with making them, that Geoghan and Bielaski, when they began working up court cases, were faced with a considerable organizational problem. The people Sapphire most wanted to convict, of course, were Reilly and Berliner, but Geoghan and Bielaski decided that it would be better policy to get a number of the less important—and less difficult—cases disposed of first. They resolved that Sapphire and Davidoff should be tried for the Bernstein fire—Mrs. Bernstein had been promised immunity; Moscowitz and Sapphire tried for the Moscowitz non-fire; Sapphire, a couple of lumber yard proprietors and the Reilly & Berliner employee who listened through the wall of the Brownsville fire house tried for a large lumber yard fire Sapphire had made, and Sapphire and a certain hosiery jobber whose place Sapphire had burned, tried for that fire. By the middle of September Geoghan was ready to prosecute all these cases. There was only one hitch. Davidoff was still missing.

Then, at the beginning of October, this last problem resolved itself. Through a seedy friend of his who kept in touch with the world situation, Sam Samuels heard that Davidoff was staying with friends in Pittsburgh. He and another National Board man boarded a train and arrived there on the morning of Yom Kippur. Samuels made straight for the Rumanian synagogue. He arrived outside the synagogue during a mid-morning break in the services.

A good many of the worshipers were getting a breath of air on the sidewalk. Samuels asked a few friendly questions and learned that Davidoff was indeed within. He sent in word that he was waiting in the street. Davidoff came out immediately. He threw his arms around Samuels, kissed him on both cheeks and burst into tears. With complete docility he permitted himself to be carried away, although Samuels had no legal authority to make him quit Pittsburgh. On the train back the second agent insisted on confiscating Davidoff's trousers when Davidoff climbed into his upper berth for the night, but even that precaution was obviously unnecessary. Davidoff appeared to be ready to confess his crimes, and Geoghan probably would have been willing to give him immunity, as he had Rose Bernstein. Before seeing the district attorney however, Davidoff had the misfortune to consult with his lawyer son, a shrewd operator. Young Davidoff persuaded his father to say not a word to the grand jury. As a result Davidoff was indicted with Sapphire for the Bernstein fire. At the trial he admitted everything, and was convicted. When he heard the verdict he wept again. As soon as his trial ended, the trial of Moscowitz and Sapphire began. Moscowitz, too, had refused to testify for the grand jury, but he was obviously in an unbalanced state. His association with firebugs had unstrung him completely; as a small child he had been in a fire, to which he owed his streaked complexion, and which had killed his mother. In his case the jury recommended mercy. The lumber yard trial followed immediately, and the hosiery trial came right after that. Both of them also resulted in convictions for all hands. Sapphire was the star witness at all these trials, as well as the ones that followed.

Meanwhile, between court appearances, Sapphire had

reluctantly implicated his old friend Irving Jaffe so thoroughly that the Manhattan District Attorney was only waiting for a lull in the Brooklyn proceedings to start trying Jaffe and four of the characters with whom he had done business, including the Mr. Horowitz who had taken part in the Rosencrantz affair. Horowitz, incidentally, provided a lamentable example of a man who put his eggs in too many different baskets. He was tried for a fire that he had helped arrange in an underwear factory; on the day Sapphire had made that fire Horowitz had been in Washington attending Roosevelt's first inaugural. While there he had apparently wangled himself the promise of a job in the Bureau of Internal Revenue. The disclosure of his incendiary activities put a rapid end to his projected career as a New Dealer.

As a result of Sapphire's implicating Irving Jaffe, Irving Jaffe ultimately implicated another clever and respected mechanic named Max Jaffe (no relation of Irving's) and Max and several of his cohorts were put out of business. In addition, the investigations inspired by Sapphire into the affairs of O'Toole, McClanahan, Schultz, Goldman & Berliner turned up a band of half a dozen Italian arsonists (Sapphire was a specialist in burning Jewish businesses), headed by a fellow who for a while had done some adjusting for the firm, and they were locked up too. Presently the district attorneys in Queens, Nassau and Bergen counties were galvanized into action by Sapphire's tales, and secured a couple of convictions each. Altogether Sapphire's decision to talk resulted in thirty convictions for arson in 1933, 1934 and 1935. In Brooklyn in 1932 (the most incendiary year in the borough's history) there had not been a single one.

8 *A doctor, a dairy and a denouement*

Bielaski was gratified of course, to see this motley crew get what was coming to it, but his consuming interest, like Sapphire's, was to convict Reilly and Berliner, whom he regarded as the fountainheads of arson in the city, and he devoted a good deal of effort to establishing all the facts pertinent to two fires that he hoped would implicate the partners. One, which Sapphire had made in the offices of a Dr. Jerome Garber, was to be used as the basis of the case against Berliner. The other, which Sapphire had made in the dairy of a woman named Lena, was the one with which he hoped to polish off Reilly.

Dr. Garber was a gay and handsome young man who had been graduated from the University of Maryland medical school in 1924. In 1928 he moved to Brooklyn and set up a workmen's compensation clinic, a form of practice not universally admired in the profession since it occasionally consists of falsely certifying that workmen have been injured on the job in return for a percentage of their compensation checks. The clinic failed in 1930, and Garber was left with several hundred dollars in unpaid debts. They remained unpaid. In 1931 Garber's father rented a four-story house on Henry Street in Brooklyn Heights, and set his son up on the parlor floor, perhaps as an abortionist, although no one ever bothered to check too closely, since arson, not illegal operations, was the subject at hand. Dr. Hess used the top floor, presumably for the same line of work. Also in 1931 Garber met Berliner, at a testimonial dinner in Berliner's honor at the Beau Rivage in Sheepshead Bay. Berliner proposed Garber as a member of the Borough Hall Boys, and the two men became rather friendly. Garber was broadminded enough to be willing to prescribe for diseases other than unintentional pregnancy, and Berliner gave him a bit of medical business. Berliner was one of the few people who did, though, and by the winter of 1932, Garber moodily came to the conclusion that he was going to go out of business again. One day he told Berliner his troubles. Berliner, the supersalesman, made his usual suggestion. Garber was horrified. He didn't mind indulging in a spot of malpractice now and then, but arson was way outside his field. "Don't be silly," said Berliner. "People are doing it every day." Garber was not difficult to persuade.

Peddling fires is apparently pretty much the same sort of exercise in applied psychology as peddling more orthodox goods or services. The most telling point Berliner made with Garber was that he could get it for him wholesale. Garber's fire, Berliner said, was really worth a thousand dollars. But, he said, Garber was a dear personal friend and if he really wanted the fire he could have it for two hundred. It was unnecessary to mention to an honorable man like Garber, Berliner said, that O'Toole, McClanahan, Schultz, Goldman and Berliner would appreciate any small favors in return, such as being given the loss to adjust. And although Sam Sapphire, the mechanic, Berliner said, was also a dear personal friend who would do anything for a friend of Berliner's, it would be tactful, perhaps, not to tell him about the six thousand dollar insurance policy carried by Garber on his office equipment, but merely to mention that the other furnishings in the house were insured for four thousand. Toward the middle of April, 1932, these details having been agreed on to the mutual satisfaction of both parties, Berliner sent Sapphire over to Henry Street to reconnoiter. Garber showed him over the house and Sapphire, after studying the layout with a critical air, stated that in his opinion the job could be done with a great deal more efficiency if certain instrument cabinets and office furniture belonging to Dr. Hess, on the top floor, were moved into Garber's office. There was no need, Garber and Sapphire agreed, to burden Dr. Hess, a busy man, with the news of this unimportant rearrangement of the furniture. The night of April 27-28 (Saturday-Sunday) was set as the time of the fire, since at that time Garber's father was planning to be in Monticello for a vacation, and Hess would also be out of town. On the afternoon of April 27, Garber carried his insurance policies to Berliner's office, as a precaution against their being burned and as a pledge of his intention to give his loss to O'Toole, McClanahan. Sapphire was there, with a black suitcase, and in Berliner's presence Garber gave him one hundred dollars in bills. Garber than took him back to Henry Street. Bridget, the doctor's maid, was sent home and told to return Monday morning. This was obviously a necessary move, but it was an indiscreet one, since Bridget's customary Saturday night orders were to stand by to take telephone calls until Garber returned. Sapphire, Garber and Garber's brother went up to Dr. Hess's offices and lugged his instrument cabinet and examining table down the two flights of stairs. Garber gave Sapphire the key to the front door, and left to keep a date with a girl. His brother left too. Sapphire opened the black suitcase and laid a train of the scrap celluloid it contained through Garber's office and examining room. He took a candle from his pocket, carefully trimmed it down so it would expire at 1 A.M., placed it on the celluloid, lit it and departed, locking the front door behind him. The alarm was turned in at 1:07. Sapphire strolled up the block as the engines arrived, glanced casually at the house and saw the fire had done what he had intended it to do, and went home. Garber got back to the house at about four, staggering slightly, and went to bed. His living quarters, on the second floor, above his offices and under Hess's, had only been singed.

He was awakened at eight o'clock by a clamor in the street. He dressed and went downstairs and discovered why Berliner had been so anxious to get his hands on the insurance policies the day before. Clustered around the front door was the usual group of howling adjusters. Berliner, craftily looking as eager as everyone else, was in the crowd. Garber allowed Berliner to collar him, and the rest of the adjusters dispersed, muttering angry, and not inaccurate, conjectures as to how O'Toole, McClanahan managed to get so much business. When Garber had concluded his arrangements with Berliner, he went back into the house to inspect the damage. His offices, he found, had been rather thoroughly burned out, but he was annoyed to discover that Hess's floor was untouched, and that the basement below his offices was only charred, like the living quarters above them. When Sapphire dropped in later in the morning to collect his other hundred, Garber expressed his dissatisfaction. Sapphire was astonished. "This looks like about a four thousand dollar fire to me," he said.

"Four thousand!" Barber blurted. "I got ten thousand."

"Ah," said Sapphire. "You should have told me. I can make ten thousand dollar jobs too." He was a man who liked to see his customers happy, though, and besides he wanted that second hundred dollars, so he took Garber to a friend of his, Jake Popkin, who sold medical equipment, old and new, on Second Avenue in Manhattan. Garber, with Sapphire's help, selected some two hundred dollars worth of rusty, battered doctor's tools. Popkin wrote two bills, one for $612.75 and one for $1437.50, describing these items as new. He dated the bills June 15, 1931 and October 10, 1931, stamped them paid, and gave them to Garber. Sapphire and the doctor returned to Henry Street with the packages, and carried them into the burned out office. Sapphire took a hammer, and beat the instruments into even worse shape than they had been in before. He produced a blow torch and charred them up a bit. Then he put them in the remains of the cabinets, and Garber gave him his money. Apparently the insurance company never questioned the planted tools, and Garber got $3150 for the fire, but that was almost a thousand dollars less than he owed, and later in the year he went into bankruptcy. His father got $850 for the damage to the stuff on the other floors. It was, as Sapphire had intended it to be, a four-thousand-dollar job, to the penny.

When Dr. Hess showed up a couple of days after the fire, and examined his office, he did not bother to conceal his feelings. In the words of a witness to the scene, "he cursed Dr. Garber and called him vile names, and he called him a dirty dog." He was not mollified, during his interview with Garber, by a telephone call from Bridget who reported that she had come to work Monday morning and had been told by Garber to go back home and await the check for back wages which he would send her. She was still waiting, she said. Hess sent her the check. For a year Hess tried to collect from Garber for his equipment, but he got nowhere. He even went so far as to file suit in Supreme Court, but before the case got on the calendar, Garber had been convicted of arson, and the matter had to be dropped. Hess's practice was considerably more thriving than Garber's had ever been, so he was able to take his loss, but he didn't like it. Garber, at the end of 1932, went to work as an assistant to a Greenwich Village practitioner, and it was at the latter's offices that the detectives went on November 18, 1933, to arrest him. They found him hiding in a closet. Five days later Berliner was arrested at his restaurant. The next day both he and Garber were indicted for second degree arson (burning an unoccupied dwelling in the nighttime or an occupied one by daylight). The trial began in County Court before the late Judge Franklin Taylor on January 2, 1934. Both Berliner and Garber pleaded not guilty when the trial opened, but at the end of the first day, when the jury had been selected, Garber suddenly changed his plea to guilty, so that the trial was of Berliner alone. Garber and Sapphire both testified at length for the prosecution, as did Bridget, Hess, Popkin and various other witnesses who were able to connect Berliner with either Garber or Sapphire. One of the unusual features of the trial was Popkin's explanation of his habit of writing phony bills. Very often, he said, a young fellow gets out of medical school, and his mother-in-law gives him a couple of thousand dollars to set up an office. So, Popkin asked, if such a young fellow, instead of spending two thousand for new stuff, could pick up used stuff for seven hundred and fifty and keep a few dollars for himself, why should he, Popkin, be unpleasant about it? The two major points made by the defense were, first, that sufficient untainted evidence of Berliner's implication in the fire had not been brought forward to corroborate the testimony of the admitted accomplices, and second that Berliner was a man of undoubted respectability whereas his principal accusers were, on their own word, characters of the shadiest sort. The trial ended the afternoon of January 4. The jury was unable to reach a verdict before bedtime, and was locked up for the night in the Towers Hotel. On the morning of the 5th, Berliner was declared guilty. He appealed the verdict all the way to the Court of Appeals, but was turned down at each step. Judge Taylor, who had long been regarded in legal circles as one of the most unpredictable of jurists, dismayed not only the defense, but the prosecution also, by sentencing Berliner to 12½ to 25 years in prison, the maximum penalty under the statute. He shocked them even more by sentencing Garber to 7 to 20 years, despite pleas for leniency on his behalf by the District Attorney, the Fire Marshal and Bielaski. Garber collapsed and had to be carried from the courtroom when he heard the sentence.

The Lena fire, which Sapphire made a month before the Garber job, was pretty much a standard operation. Lena's Dairy was a small establishment in a taxpayer on King's Highway. The price for the job had been set by Sapphire at $200, and Lena had given him $100 cash and a note for $100. Two or three days after the fire he had sold her back the note for $50 cash, which she had borrowed from her brother-in-law. She had collected $1937.22 which, as usual, had not been enough to cover her debts. O'Toole, McClanahan had adjusted the loss. The point of dispute in the case was whether Reilly had sent Sapphire to Lena, as Sapphire insisted, or whether he hadn't, as he maintained. Lena herself was a particularly hardboiled specimen, with black hair, a ruddy complexion and a rude tongue. She was first questioned immediately after Sapphire's arrest, and denied everything. Some months later the District Attorney finally agreed to let her testify before the Grand Jury without signing a waiver of immunity, and she admitted that Sapphire had made the fire for her. She still declared Reilly had had nothing to do with it. Finally, during one of the prolonged questionings to which she was subjected, Fire Marshal Brophy thought of investigating the contents of her purse. In it, he testified at the trial, he found one of Reilly's business cards with "Lena" scribbled across it in pencil. "My God," said Brophy, "that's Reilly's writing." Since Reilly, in the time he had worked for the Fire Marshal, had been a sort of secretary, keeping the daily records of the office, Brophy was, presumably, well acquainted with his penmanship. Confronted with this damning disclosure, Lena changed her story to say that Reilly had arranged the fire, and had told her that the mechanic, when he came, would bear just such a card. Sapphire had brought that card to her, she said, and she had put it in her handbag and forgotten all about it. Brophy personally arrested his old aide. The card, of course, was the key piece of evidence at Reilly's trial, and there was much bickering among handwriting experts, and much questioning of Lena as to how many handbags she owned, how often she examined their contents and so forth. She stuck to her story, though, and in the end Reilly was convicted. The Appellate Division upheld the verdict, but the Court of Appeals found an error in Judge

Taylor's charge. The judge, despite repeated demands by defense counsel, had neglected to point out to the jury that no evidence had been introduced to show that Reilly had any knowledge that the building housing Lena's store —as opposed to the contents of the store itself—had been insured. At his second trial Reilly was acquitted. In 1936 the insurance companies lowered their rates for Brooklyn.

Judge Taylor had sentenced Berliner and Reilly (also 12½ to 25) in March, 1934, and two or three of the minor offenders, including Moscowitz, whose sentence he had suspended, he had sentenced early in 1935. On September 23, 1935, the remainder of the Brooklyn arsonists were brought before him. It was then that he gave Garber his 7 to 20 years. Davidoff got 10 to 25. In contrast, Irving Jaffe, in Manhattan, had gotten 3½ years, which was a stiff sentence according to usual practice. About Sapphire Judge Taylor said, "His sentence must be written in letters so large that he who runs may read. . . . The chair would be a suitable answer for his nefarious deeds." And he gave him 20 to 40 years, the maximum sentence for first degree arson (burning an inhabited dwelling by night), despite his two years of labor for the state. Of that time Sapphire actually served 11 years and four months, two years less than what the complete sentence would have amounted to with the customary allowance for good behavior. Throughout this time Bielaski and Ralph K. Jacobs, who had been the assistant district attorney who had actually tried the Brooklyn cases, attempted to get him out. That they finally succeeded was due to the fact that Sapphire's two youngest sons had both been decorated for valor during the war. Their pleas for their father as they stood before Governor Thomas E. Dewey in their bemedaled uniforms, had been impossible to turn down. Of all the participants in Brooklyn arson plots, Baby emerged as the most admirable. Through those eleven years, during all of which she was impoverished, and during most of which she was ill, she took care of Sapphire's children, and visited him regularly. When he got out, the parole authorities refused to let him live with her because her husband was still stubbornly opposed to a divorce, so Bielaski, who knows a bit about hanky-panky himself, shipped her off to Mexico for a couple of months, and she returned an honorable woman in the eyes of the Parole Board. She and Sapphire were promptly married. Sapphire had a difficult time in Clinton Prison because of his reputation as a squealer. He became so depressed by his environment at one point that he shammed a fit of insanity so he could get a little rest in the prison hospital. He got into the prison hospital all right, but it took him more than a year to persuade the authorities he wasn't really crazy so they would let him out. He was not the most philosophical convict who ever served time; his letters to Bielaski, of which he wrote scores, were invariably querulous. In one of them he wrote, "The time is getting shorter and my heart is growing weaker and colder and these few lines are not mere Shakespearean quotes." Shortly after he did get out, and was just on the point of finding some occupation that would earn a living for Baby and himself, he had a severe heart attack, which permanently prevented him from doing any full time work. He remained, though, recognizably Sam Sapphire. He paid a call on Bielaski not long ago, to tell him the latest gossip about Brooklyn arson, and to ask him for a loan, and went out with him to a luncheonette for a cup of coffee. The check came to twenty cents. Sapphire insisted on paying it. As they got up from the counter, he took an extra quarter from his pocket and slid it over to the waitress.

PART TWO

Elias Eliopoulos

1 *Concerning an old, old business*

Although its present repute, like that of another business of undoubted antiquity, is low, the manufacture, distribution and sale of narcotic drugs, especially opium and its derivatives, is an ancient and honorable branch of commerce. Sumerian ideograms dating back to 4000 B.C. describe the opium poppy as the "plant of joy"; Egyptian papyri notice opium, and so do Assyrian medical tablets taken from the library of King Assurbanipal. Homer, Virgil and Plutarch mention opium in their writings, and such eminent medicos as Hippocrates and Galen speak of it enthusiastically as a pain killer. The drug, in fact, has been an indispensable part of the pharmacopoeia of every civilized nation for upward of two thousand years, and it still is. Its immense pharmaceutical potency, however, is also the reason it has so often been abused. There have always been opium addicts, drawn largely from two classes of people: chronic invalids who found in the drug their only sure relief from pain, and disoriented characters who chose the raptures of permanent intoxication over the less elevated pleasures of occasional sobriety. Among the more prominent opium eaters of recent times were

Samuel Taylor Coleridge, Edgar Allan Poe and, of course, Thomas De Quincey. Drug addiction was a relatively difficult state to attain, however, until the nineteenth century, when scientific research began to make so many things easy. In 1803 a French chemist isolated morphine, the alkaloid base of opium, which is about six times as powerful as the drug in its crude state. Morphine was an extremely valuable addition to the pharmacopoeia, and its use rapidly became widespread. Then, in 1853, a Scotch doctor invented the hypodermic syringe, which made dosage more accurate and the effect of the drug more rapid. Medical opinion greeted this new method of administering morphine delightedly; morphine addiction was beginning to become a worrisome medical problem, and doctors believed that since the drug, when injected, did not enter the stomach, addiction, or "appetite," for it would be eliminated by the new technique. The first person known to have died of excessive morphinism due to hypodermic injection of the drug was the Scotch doctor's wife. So gleefully did the medical profession take to passing out shots in the arm, that during the Civil War in this country addiction to morphine became known as the "Army disease." It took only a few years for doctors to realize that the subcutaneous administration of morphine was no less dangerous than oral dosage, but all their efforts to control use of the drug were of no avail because there were no laws governing its distribution. Pharmacies everywhere sold opium, morphine and hypodermic syringes freely; in the United States almost every patented "Pain Killer"—and there were hundreds of them—contained opium in some form, and so did most patented cures for opium addiction. The climax to this desperate state of affairs came in 1898 when a German chemist treated morphine with acetic acid and came up with diacetylmorphine, a white powder that is inhaled like snuff. He was so proud of this contribution to peace and progress that he named it heroin. If only because heroin is a good deal more powerful than morphine and a great deal less unpleasant to take, its appearance would have stimulated addiction; in addition, doctors once again distinguished themselves by proclaiming it non-habit forming and, in fact, an excellent cure for the morphine habit. In 1903 the United States imported 350 tons of raw opium and about 800 pounds of morphine and other opium derivatives. These days, with the strict controls that are maintained, 100 tons of opium a year is considered ample for all purposes including the manufacture of morphine. No morphine is imported at all, and heroin has been stricken from the U. S. Pharmacopoeia although it is still used in other countries.

The precise nature of "addiction" to opium—or to anything else—is still something of a moot point. The majority of legislators, clergymen, judges and policemen are inclined to regard it, apparently, as a purely physiological state, caused directly by some demonic quality inherent in the drug, and indirectly by the all-around unreliability of human nature. According to this view anyone who, after taking a first nibble, does not plunge headlong down the road to perdition must be a person of unusual moral stamina. Many doctors, however, doubt that any habit is entirely physical, and are persuaded that acute drug addiction, like acute alcoholism, say, is a vivid symptom of an individual's mental illness. A person with a healthy psyche, they maintain, would be unlikely to become an addict even if heroin were to be had by the bucketful at every corner drugstore. Whatever the rights and wrongs of this dispute may be, it is certainly true that the thoroughgoing opium addict is about as pitiable a spectacle as the world can afford. Even if he could, while under the influence, produce a regular succession of works as good as "Kubla Khan," his condition would not be one to be encouraged. The first phases of addiction are delightful. Opium acts on the brain in such a way as to deaden sensations of pain or weariness; in someone unaccustomed to the drug it produces, besides, a state of positive exaltation. "The opium eater," says De Quincey, "feels that the diviner part of his nature is paramount —that is, the moral affections are in a state of cloudless serenity, and high over all [is] the great light of the majestic intellect." De Quincey took crude opium rather than morphine or heroin; he took it orally rather than subcutaneously or nasally; and he was a man with sufficient powers of will to be able to abstain entirely from the drug for a period of several months four different times during his life. His moral affections, therefore, were cloudlessly serene for considerably longer periods than those enjoyed by an ordinary drug addict. With daily doses of morphine or heroin, a person who is so inclined can become addicted in a matter of weeks, and, once he is, the positive effects of the drug dwindle until his dose no longer makes paramount the diviner part of his nature, but merely prevents him from being uncomfortable. Meanwhile he has begun to experience the "withdrawal," or abstinence, symptoms. The sufferings of an opium addict deprived of his drug include almost every unpleasant symptom known to medical science. First of all he begins to itch and to fidget; then he starts yawning and sneezing, his eyes water and his nose runs; his fidgeting becomes a pronounced palsy of the limbs; he suffers racking chills; he develops an acute distaste for food. That's just the beginning. Presently he becomes really sick: he sweats profusely, has diarrhea, vomits continually, and can't sleep; he gets abdominal cramps and severe pains in his joints; and, at the same time, he is still itching, yawning and sneezing, his eyes are still watering, his hands are still shaking, and any small discomfort—a lumpy mattress, a pin scratch, an unkind word—is a source of almost unbearable anguish to him. He begins babbling deliriously of suicide, and undoubtedly would be glad to do away with himself if he only had the energy. A major part of his agony is the positive knowledge that just one little dose of his drug—but nothing else on earth—would put him out of all his misery immediately. He becomes completely prostrated. These symptoms in their acute stage persist for two or three days. For another week or ten days they slacken off; then they recur intermittently for months. It may be years before an ex-addict ceases to be acutely sensitive to unimportant annoyances, and a symptom that often persists indefinitely is insomnia. Such sleep as an ex-addict does get is crowded with dreadful nightmares. It is not surprising, therefore, that a thoroughgoing opium addict is able to have only one purpose in life, to maintain his supply of the drug, and that he should pursue this end with extraordinary resolution and to the exclusion of any other activity. Once the New York police found a morphine addict starving to death in the street with forty dollars in his pocket; he had resolved many years before never to be without at least that much cash for drugs. One of the most common occurrences in hospitals where addiction is cured is for an addict to present himself voluntarily, begging piteously for a cure, with several ounces of the drug concealed on his person.

Since this kind of addiction among its citizens is a condition that few responsible governments desire to encourage, in most of the world the traffic in narcotic drugs, during the last fifty years, has become subjected to stringent official control. And since it is axiomatic that every new law or regulation automatically creates new crimes, it has been inevitable that the narcotics trade should have become a rewarding field of operations for criminals. In accordance with a corollary to the axiom, in fact, the tighter the controls have been, the more rewarding the trade. There have been some truly gigantic conspiracies to traffic in narcotics since the turn of the century and of these the largest and most successful of all flourished between 1927 and 1932, during which time it penetrated to almost every corner of the earth, under the truly inspired leadership of a distinguished Greek merchant named Elias Konstantin Eliopoulos.

2 *Elias's resources wane*

The Piraeus, where Elias was born on February 11, 1894, owes its existence to the fact that Athens is inconveniently located inland; almost its sole function is to serve as the capital's seaport, and its life pretty much revolves around international commerce, a field of endeavor in which no one is seriously handicapped by having sharp wits and a dull conscience. Elias, who by birth and upbringing was destined for a mercantile career—his father was head of the local chamber of commerce—was amply —it might even be said excessively—endowed with both qualities. He spent a year at Robert College, an American institution in Constantinople, and a year at the Athens University law school. Then, in 1913 he went to work as the confidential secretary to a family friend, Euripides Mavromatis, a merchant himself and a substantial one. "Merchant" in the Piraeus was an elastic term, covering almost any variety of business. Mavromatis concerned himself with import-export, with developing mining properties, with the price of grain futures, with chartering coastwise vessels, with selling insurance policies, and with lending money, to name only a few of his more easily comprehensible lines of work. An important purpose of this heterogeneous activity was to create opportunities for speculating in foreign currency, the trickiest way to make a drachma known to man. To cite a wholly fictitious example, Mavromatis would be likely to buy a Rumanian oat crop for drachmas, sell it in Budapest for pounds sterling, deposit the pounds in a Stockholm bank against a debt incurred by a purchase of German mining stock, sell the stock on the Paris Bourse for Swiss francs, convert the francs into dollars, and use the dollars to pay for an incoming shipment of rawhide from the Argentine, all inside seventy-two hours and at a fifty percent profit. It was his education in this difficult school that was responsible for Elias's subsequent success in the narcotics business. The drug traffic is the most international of all businesses, and without the comprehensive knowledge he acquired of rates of exchange, stock market regulations, steamship routes, banking procedures, and the venality of government officials, he would have been seriously handicapped as a trafficker.

Elias worked for Mavromatis for three years. For the first two of them he also held another job, as manager of the commercial department of the Constantinople Gas Company. He left that position abruptly in 1914, and there is some reason to believe that a substantial portion of the company's assets left with him when he departed. Greek-Turkish relations being what they were in 1914, however, this could easily have been regarded, and probably was, as the inspired deed of an ardent patriot. Elias spent 1916 as a private in the Greek army. When he emerged, his uncle, also a "merchant," took him in as a partner. For about three years Elias and his uncle devoted themselves to purveying supplies to the Greek army, a venture that was extremely profitable until the currencies of Europe went into their post-war palpitations. In 1919 Elias pulled out of the business in disgust, and with his two younger brothers, George and Athanasios, set up the firm of Eliopoulos Frères, a typically unspecific enterprise. The East India trade was involved, and Balkan grain crops, and at one point Elias made an arrangement with an Akron rubber company, specializing in contraceptives, to distribute its products in the Levant. When the drachma fell disastrously in 1920, this connection was severed, however. The precise nature of Elias's business for the next five or six years is unclear, although it is certain that he scurried all over Europe transacting it. In 1924 the Rumanian police mentioned his name in connection with a neatly executed bit of forgery in Constanza (where George had taken up residence in 1920), and some time later the Bulgarian constabulary, in an unsuccessful attempt to round up members of a counterfeiting ring, issued a description that might have been of Elias. There is an old Greek proverb, after all, "You got to make a drachma to have a drachma." Despite his felonious proclivities, Elias was no uncouth ruffian, however. He was suave, dignified and gentlemanly. He wore fawn-colored spats and carried a gold-headed walking stick. He spoke English and French fluently, frequented the best hotels, and was on cordial terms with bankers and diplomats all over Europe. Thanks to a lofty forehead, an aquiline nose of noble proportions, a commanding eye and a military bearing, his presence inspired confidence and respect. His conversation was graceful and revealed a quick and accurate perception of men and affairs. Only one unfortunate circumstance prevented him from assuming a place among the shapers of Europe's destiny: As he was

to put it some years later, "In 1926 I found myself with
waning resources." In a word, he was broke.

At this unhappy moment he made the acquaintance of a
Greek named David Gourievidis, who was really a Russian named David Gourevich. Gourievidis, an unctuous,
rat-faced little man, was a spat-wearer himself, although
at one time in his career he had been a resident of a Si-
berian salt mine. Just where his encounter with Elias took
place is obscure, although where it didn't take place is
fairly clear; one of the conditions under which Gourievidis had been granted Greek citizenship, apparently, had
been that under no circumstances whatever was he to set
foot in Greece. His profession was narcotics smuggler, his
market was the Orient, and at the time of his meeting
with Elias, he, also, found himself with waning resources.
Believing Elias to be a man of substance, he spoke elo-
quently of the rewards that could be obtained by interesting oneself in morphine and heroin—providing, of course,
one had some capital to invest. Elias was impressed, and
early in 1927 he and Gourievidis set out for China to
look the situation over. They went by ship—Gourievidis,
fearful that in some quarters he might still be regarded
as Gourevich, was unwilling to risk the Trans-Siberian
Railroad—and so the journey took several weeks, ample
time for Gourievidis to explain some of the intricacies of
his business to Elias. The drug business, Gourievidis told
Elias, was set up very much like any other business; manufacturers disposed of their product to large distributors,
the distributors arranged for the merchandise to be
shipped to wholesalers in various parts of the world, the
wholesalers dealt with local jobbers and the jobbers sold
to the retailers. The only contact an addict had with the
traffic, Gourievidis said, was with his retailer, an inconse-
quential hoodlum, usually, who dealt in drugs by the

gram. Gourievidis was a distributor, purchasing drugs in lots of a hundred kilograms or more from European manufacturers, and sending them to wholesalers in China. He never had the slightest contact with addicts, the ultimate consumers of his merchandise, and seldom even saw the drugs themselves. He was simply a respectable business man, he said, who negotiated with factory sales managers, made arrangements with forwarding companies, exchanged telegrams with his associates in the Orient, made deposits and withdrawals at various banks, and generally attended to work that was performed on typewriters, telephones and calculating machines. Many retailers of drugs were addicts, he said, but no one who held a position of any importance in the traffic was so stupid as to use drugs himself.

Elias was curious about the risks that a narcotics trafficker ran, and Gourievidis was loquacious on this point too. The risks were very slight for a man in his position, he pointed out, because, although the traffic itself was international, the statutes designed to control it were strictly local. Some countries had severe laws about dealing in drugs, some had lenient laws, and some had no laws at all. Even those countries that had severe laws generally covered only importation and sale in their legislation; practically nowhere was the manufacture of narcotics restricted, or was export controlled. The big trick, Gourievidis pointed out, was never to sell drugs in the same country that you bought them in; never, if possible, to enter the country you sold them in, and never to have dealings at all in the country of which you were a citizen. Anyhow, he added, six months in prison was regarded as a pretty stiff sentence for a narcotics offense in most European countries, so what could you lose? Elias had never undergone penal servitude in a salt mine, and so he did

not share Gourievidis's bland attitude toward milder
forms of incarceration. Otherwise, though, he thought
the project sounded promising, and any lingering doubts
he might have had about it were dispelled when he
reached Tientsin and was introduced to a broadshoul-
dered, sun-tanned countryman of his, John D. Voyatzis.
Voyatzis, in the guise of a coffee and tobacco importer,
had been living merrily in the French Concession for
twenty-five years. He was one of the principal importers
of drugs in China, and had made a fortune without ever
having been molested for a moment. Elias was not yet
in a financial position to enter into any specific arrangements with Voyatzis, but the two men got along well and
Elias, after conversing with Voyatzis for several days, and
meeting a number of other characters connected with the
trade, was eager to return to Europe and raise the money
necessary to become their colleague. Gourievidis traveled with him, and they decided that Paris was the most
likely place to commence operations. There, Gourievidis
introduced Elias to a couple of French drug manufacturers, and to another Frenchman, a former card sharp and
confidence man, who had become a prominent entrepre-
neur in the narcotics field. This Frenchman had best be
identified simply as J——, since in recent years he has
won not only complete forgiveness for past misbehavior,
but also membership in the Légion d'Honneur for valuable work during the Resistance. J—— was the proprietor
of a restaurant and café much frequented by Gestapo
officers during the occupation, and he was able to hear
a good deal of useful gossip. He was also in a position,
when he came across a particularly savage German, to slip
a lethal dose of heroin into his champagne. A grateful
nation felt that no purpose would be served by inquiring
too deeply into where J—— got the heroin.

Just as Elias, in 1927, was busy improving his relations with J—— and other acquaintances of Gourievidis, he learned that Dr. Rodrigo Morejon Lobera, a South American acquaintance of weak intellect and large resources, was in town. Knowing the source of a grubstake when he saw one, Elias called on Dr. Lobera and told him that for half a million francs (about twenty thousand dollars) he could purchase two hundred kilograms (440 pounds) of morphine in Germany. Dr. Lobera gladly turned the money over to Elias, and also loaned him his automobile for the trip. Elias and Gourievidis motored to Germany and secured the drugs. When they were safely back across the French border they stopped, took the morphine out of the car, overturned the car, and set it on fire. They made the rest of the trip back to Paris by train, and presented themselves to Lobera, haggard and disheveled, clutching some charred cardboard which they claimed was all that was left of the morphine. Then, together with J—— and an elderly Chilean ex-jewel robber named Leonoff-Goldstein, both of whom had assisted in the plot, they divided up the drugs. When Elias had disposed of his share he found himself with 200,000 francs cash, enough to go into business. He immediately returned to China, without Gourievidis this time, to conclude arrangements with Voyatzis. In Tientsin Voyatzis appointed Elias his Paris purchasing agent, and advanced funds for the first few purchases. Elias got back to Paris in May, 1928, set himself up in an apartment near the Eiffel Tower, and notified his brother Athanasios, in Athens, that at last the affairs of Eliopoulos Frères had taken a turn for the better.

Oddly enough, the work Elias had contracted to do for Voyatzis was quite legal. Almost anyone could obtain a license to manufacture narcotics in France, and manufacturers could import as much raw opium as they wanted, and turn out as much heroin or morphine. The only controls that existed were over the sale of the manufactured drugs. All sales had to be made through licensed brokers, or *courtiers*, and for each transaction a *courtier* engaged in, he had to purchase a permit, or *bon de toxique*, for 25 francs. The books of the manufacturers and the *courtiers* were inspected periodically by the government. What the authorities were concerned with, however, was that no drugs were distributed to non-medical consumers inside France; they did not care a hang who bought the drugs outside the country. The importation of drugs into China, for example, was strictly illegal under Chinese law, but exporting them from France to China was, under French law, quite all right. Elias, consequently, did not even have to conceal his activities. He simply had to purchase drugs through a *courtier*—of whom there were some 325, many of them exceptionally shady in character—and send them off. Getting them into China was Voyatzis's problem, and since all attempts to enforce the anti-narcotics laws there were regarded by the populace with the same sort of enthusiasm that Americans were then displaying toward the Eighteenth Amendment, it wasn't much of a problem.

As of the first day of 1929 the situation in France changed somewhat, but not enough to curtail Elias's activities seriously. In 1925 the League of Nations had adopted a convention setting up a uniform system for the control of the international flow of narcotics. In brief, it provided for a system of import and export licenses for all shipments. The exporting country was charged with making certain that the importing country had issued an import license before it was empowered to grant an export license. This convention was not ratified by the necessary number of countries until 1928, at which time the French government promulgated a series of laws to conform to it, and announced that they would go into effect on the first of the new year. The months of November and December, 1928, were a period of feverish activity for the traffickers, but shortly after January 1, 1929, they discovered that they had wasted their energy. The French authorities were no more interested than they had ever been in the problems of other countries. The traffickers continued to inform the authorities of their shipments, but the information was conveyed unofficially, now, and the shipments were manifested as dried peas, painters' colors, kid gloves or any other article of merchandise that seemed amusing, and would protect the French government from appearing to flout the Convention. Falsifying factory books and *bons de toxique,* proved very little of a problem either, since the inspectors who examined them were generally superannuated apothecaries, quivering with age and weariness. After January 1, 1929, Elias's activities, of course, had no longer the slightest odor of legality, but this did not seem to trouble him greatly.

It is not difficult to understand why Elias was an immediate and luminous success in the drug traffic. The personnel of the traffic, on the whole, consisted of characters like Gourievidis, the ex-Siberian convict; J——, the ex-card sharp; and Leonoff-Goldstein, the ex-jewel robber, to name three of the more distinguished members of the fraternity. Such gentlemen as these were well versed in all the ways of making a dishonest living, but few of them had had any training in making an honest one, as Elias had had. Elias's grasp of the fundamentals of legitimate commerce marked him at once as a born leader. He set about establishing himself in his new business with as much method as if he had been the most reputable of capitalists. He proceeded on the assumption that the key to power in the drug traffic was control of the sources of supply. With that in mind he focussed his attention on the two most susceptible drug companies he knew, the Comptoir des Alcaloides at Noisy-le-Sec, which was owned in part by one L——, a Frenchman who has since reformed, and the Societé Industrielle de Chimie Organique, or SICO as it was called, at Ste. Genevieve, operated by an unprincipled Belgian named Paul Mechelaere. Both concerns, of course, were perfectly open, legal ones, as the French law stood at the time, but this legality was due rather to good luck than to good intentions, since almost their entire output was quite frankly going to the illicit traffic in other countries. Elias's technique for securing the control of the product of the two factories was in the classic tradition of free enterprise: It consisted simply of demanding more drugs from them than they could conveniently supply, and offering them such attractive prices that they gladly accepted his financial backing in order to expand their facilities. He was able to pull this operation off successfully because of Voyatzis's enormous, almost insatiable, requirements for the Chinese market. It has been estimated that the annual world need for morphine for legitimate medical purposes is 100 tons. China alone, in the late twenties, was consuming morphine at the rate of five tons a year, and equal quantities of heroin were being sent there at the same time. The major problem faced by SICO and the Comptoir in endeavoring to supply Elias was their inability to pay for the huge amounts of raw opium they needed to manufacture the drugs. (One pound of opium makes about two ounces of morphine.) Opium is the kind of merchandise that is not easily obtained on credit, particularly by people like L—— and Mechelaere, and credit was all they had on hand. What Elias did was to advance the two concerns enough cash to buy opium, in return for a lien on the as yet unmanufactured drugs. By the beginning of 1929 he had virtually cornered the narcotics market in France. Anyone who wanted drugs of French manufacture had to get them from or through Elias—which, of course, was not the most difficult thing in the world to do.

Elias was not able to manage this extensive a business without assistance. At the same time that he was gaining control of the drug factories, he was building an organization of his own, although it would be unsafe to attempt to describe with any degree of precision just how this organization was set up. Not long ago an authority on the drug traffic was asked if he could give a lucid account of the traffic's administrative structure, and of the relationships of its various members to one another. "Did you ever try," he said, "to draw an organizational chart of a plateful of spaghetti? That's what the traffic's like. You know that every piece touches every other piece somewhere, but damned if you know just where." Elias's set-up was particularly spaghetti-like. He rapidly won recognition as the most powerful figure in the traffic, and at one time or another he had dealings with just about every other trafficker of any consequence in the world, but it would be impossible to say just how long and for what purposes any specific person was on his payroll, with the exception of half a dozen minor scoundrels who were permanent employees, and, of course, his two brothers—Athanasios, or Nasso, as everyone called him, and George—with whom he hastened to share his good fortune. George had established himself in a particularly favorable spot for opening a branch office of a narcotics company, Constanza, Rumania's biggest seaport, where for a number of years he had sulkily occupied himself with the insurance business. His sulkiness was the outcome of a bitter family quarrel. George had been married in 1921 to the daughter of that very Euripides Mavromatis for whom Elias had worked before the war. In 1923 Mavromatis's other daughter had become engaged to Nasso. Nasso had jilted her, leaving her in a condition that was extremely interesting to her neighbors, but not to her. This, not unnaturally, had led to some vehement conversations between Nasso and Mavromatis. George was forced to side with his wife's father, of course. Elias, with his genius for supporting the felonious side of every question, took Nasso's part. George had withdrawn from Eliopoulos Frères in 1923 and had not spoken to either of his brothers since, until Elias, looking sleek, showed up in Constanza one day in 1928, and raised the question of narcotics. His bank accounts were impressive enough, even then, to erase such a relatively small matter as a misused sister-in-law from George's mind. He undertook to handle the Rumanian end of Eliopoulos Frères, just as Nasso was managing the firm's Greek affairs from Athens.

Elias's motive for opening branch offices in Constanza and Athens was not solely to provide a living for his blood relations. He was an ambitious man who wanted to expand his business as rapidly as possible, and the Balkan countries, with their haphazard law enforcement systems and their venal civil servants, were a logical site for the activities in which he was engaged. Constanza was a particularly valuable port in which to have a representative, since it is right across the Black Sea from Turkey, and a large proportion of the raw opium brought into Europe to be converted into drugs came from Turkey or, via Turkey, from Iran. Yugoslavia, and Bulgaria, to which Constanza is also handy, are poppy-growing countries too. Another fact of a slightly less technical nature recommended Rumania to Elias. In Paris Elias had made the acquaintance of a Rumanian, a friend of King Carol's, whose unique business it was to supply diplomatic couriers to anyone who wanted contraband carried across national frontiers without any danger of its being detected by customs inspectors. Several members of the Rumanian legation in Paris offered their pouches for this sort of service, and Elias felt that since he was going to make heavy use of Rumanians to carry his merchandise for him, it would be well to have a trustworthy representative in Rumania. Elias's final—and most urgent —reason for spreading his activities into as many countries as possible was precautionary. He was very much aware that sooner or later the French government would be forced by public opinion, if not by its conscience, to proclaim effective anti-narcotic laws, and to enforce them. He did not want to be in the position of having all his sources of supply, his shipping facilities, his bank accounts and his associates together in France when that dread day arrived. He believed, quite rightly, that it would be much less hazardous, as well as more profitable, for him to be operating all over the place than in just one vicinity. By the time he reached the height of his career in 1930 and 1931, he was using almost every port in Europe to ship his merchandise out, he had representatives in Istanbul, Athens, Constanza, Hamburg, Trieste, Alexandria, New York, Shanghai, Tientsin and probably a dozen other ports, and he had bank accounts in London, Berne, Paris, Athens, Berlin and several other cities. He used steamship lines of every flag; diplomatic couriers from Rumania, Peru and Afghanistan; and the personnel of his enterprises, from a national point of view, was as motley as possible although there always did seem to be a preponderance of Greeks.

4 *From the Pyramids to Legs Diamond by diplomatic pouch*

Meanwhile it had come to the attention of Elias and J——
that their old buddy, Dr. Lobera, still had some money
left, a deplorable situation from their point of view. They
promptly took steps to correct their oversight. After apologizing profusely for their previous mishap, they told
Lobera that they were prepared to make amends. They
had learned, they told him, that a certain El Raschid in
Cairo had a vast supply of heroin for sale, and that a
little on-the-spot negotiating might make them all rich.
Lobera again rose to the bait, and in January, 1929, a
gay little traveling party consisting of Lobera, J—— and
his wife, Elias and a French alkaloid chemist named An-
dré Christophe, set off for Cairo. When they arrived at
their hotel there, they were greeted by a character in a
morning coat and fez who introduced himself as El
Raschid, but who really was one of Elias's principal hench-
men, a Greek named Kosta Belokas, who made his headquarters in Istanbul. El Raschid-Belokas gave such a
glowing account of the enormous amounts of heroin he
had in stock—hidden somewhere out in the desert, presumably—that Lobera was easily persuaded to turn a large

sum over to him. Elias, J—— and Christophe were to accompany El Raschid to the desert hideout and return with
the drugs. They disappeared, and two days later reported
to Lobera, unkempt and miserable once again, saying that
on their way back from the desert they had been set upon
by a fierce pack of camel-borne Bedouins who had stolen
the heroin, and all their cash besides. Upon hearing this
news, Lobera swooned. He was several hours coming to,
and it was a week before he felt strong enough to rise from
his bed. The money was divided equally among Elias,
J——, Christophe and Belokas. One would think that after
this shocking experience Lobera would have been able
to perceive that Elias was a dangerous man to do business
with, but the good doctor was rather obtuse, and besides
both Elias and J——, an experienced confidence man,
were profusely and plausibly apologetic, having discovered that Lobera still had 80,000 francs left. Some
months later, back in Paris, they acquired this last pitiful
sum by recruiting a fast-talking Italian who claimed to be
an expert counterfeiter. Once again, urged by J—— and
Elias, Lobera trustingly parted with his money. He never
saw any of his erstwhile associates again. This time,
knowing that they had cleaned him out, J—— and Elias
didn't even bother to account for the failure of the project. They simply cut the doctor dead, and he presently
disappeared into South American obscurity, sadder than
when he arrived, and poorer, but probably no wiser.

As a matter of fact Lobera's utter incompetence as a
crook, despite his earnest desire to be one, was forcibly
illustrated by his agreeing to go to Egypt to purchase
drugs. Egypt in the twenties was a place to sell drugs, not
to buy them. Next to China it was the most prominent
"victim country" on the globe; something like half a mil-

lion people—four percent of the population—were addicted to heroin, and the situation was made even worse by the fact that almost all of the addicts were males between the ages of twenty and forty, which meant that almost a quarter of that normally useful segment of the population was unfit for active duty, or rapidly becoming so. In addition just about everyone partook from time to time of hashish, which is marijuana in edible form. Describing Cairo in 1929, a contemporary historian wrote, "The street scene presents a picture that, for general debauchery and intoxication, looks like an oriental version of Hogarth's 'Gin Alley.'" In that year Sir Thomas Wentworth Russell, an Englishman who was Commandant of the Cairo City Police, was given the additional job of director of the Central Narcotics Intelligence Bureau. Russell Pasha, as he styled himself, was quite a figure in Egypt. He wore a tattersall vest and a turban, and he was an exceptionally able policeman. In a few months he had already ranged as far as Vienna to eliminate a gang of Austrians who were large suppliers of the Egyptian market, and he was constantly incarcerating Italian steamship stewards and Turkish rug dealers, two classes of people who seemed to have an unaccountable penchant for dealing in drugs. Elias went into business just a little too late to take full advantage of the Egyptian boom, but he did earn a franc or two there before Russell Pasha made things difficult for him. In 1928 Elias, using the name Anastasopoulos, had made connections with a pair of Swiss chemists, Dr. Fritz Müller of Basel and Dr. Hubert Rauch of Vernier. Dr. Müller had a permit to manufacture and sell narcotics; most of his sales were to Dr. Rauch, who dealt with "Anastasopoulos." The bulk of these drugs was sent in false-bottomed trunks, via Trieste, into Egypt. This cosy arrangement was brought to an abrupt halt by Russell Pasha's men a few months after it had begun, when they seized one of the trunks in Alexandria, and methodically traced the origin of the drugs back to Müller and Rauch, who were promptly arrested, tried, convicted and imprisoned by the Swiss authorities. An examination of Müller's books showed that 1563 kilograms of morphine had gone from his factory to Rauch. The name, Anastasopoulos, came up at the trial, but the authorities all believed that there was no such person, and that the name had been introduced by Rauch to make it appear that he hadn't done the smuggling himself. It was fortunate for Elias that Rauch only knew him by the assumed name, since the chemist would obviously have had no hesitation about turning him in if he had known who or where he was. Nevertheless the closing of Müller's factory was a blow to Elias, and, on the advice of Belokas, his Near Eastern expert, he decided to make a new attempt to supply Egypt. For this project he recruited Carlos Fernandez Bacula, who at the time was the Peruvian chargé d'affaires at Oslo.

Bacula was a slender, sallow man, with liquid eyes, romantic whiskers and the manners of a grandee. The admiration with which he filled women was exceeded only by the admiration with which they filled him. He had started life as a card sharp and confidence man, in which capacity he had become associated with J——, and their friendship had persisted when he became a member of his unsuspecting government's diplomatic corps, on the strength of his familiarity with Europe and his gentlemanly demeanor. His first post had been in Vienna, which was a center of the narcotics traffic, and there he had put his diplomatic pouch at the disposal of the oldest and wiliest of all European traffickers, a Pole named Stefan Tomko. When he was transferred to Oslo, he continued to flit about the globe breaking hearts and distributing morphine. It was J——, one of whose sources of income was acting as Bacula's impresario, who brought Bacula and Elias together. In the spring of 1929 J—— and Elias made a second trip to Cairo, accompanied by Bacula, who carried 250 kilograms of heroin in his diplomatic luggage, at his standard fee for a trip of that length, 10 pounds sterling a kilogram. Once again they were met by Belokas, who had discarded his fez for this occasion, and who told them that he had found a customer for the heroin in the person of a local carpet dealer who had been one of the links in the Viennese organization that Russell Pasha had abolished. The carpet dealer, however, could not afford to take such a large quantity at one time. He agreed to buy 100 kilograms and no more. After searching unsuccessfully for more customers, Elias was forced to conclude that the Egyptian market had become too constricted for him due to Russell Pasha's energetic work, and he asked Bacula to take the other 150 kilos back to France again. Bacula agreed to do it for another 10 pounds a kilo, which he was paid, and so he earned 4000 pounds for his part in the venture, a good deal more than anyone else made out of it.

Bacula, of course, did not always do that well. A good part of his income came from the American trade, with whom J—— had established both him and Elias. Bacula made several trips across the Atlantic to deliver Elias's goods to the Newman brothers, one of the important American import firms. On one occasion he arrived in New York with 150 kilograms for the Newmans, and checked into a midtown hotel where he was joined by a

Newman representative. He gave this man 50 kilos to deliver, saying he would keep the other 100 until his commission had been paid. A few hours later the man returned, bleeding copiously, and reported that the drugs had been hijacked from his car. Bacula was pondering what to do next, when his door was pushed open, and Legs Diamond walked in. Diamond said he had heard there had been some trouble, and asked if he could be of any assistance. Bacula told him about the hijacking. Diamond said he'd see what he could do, and left. He returned, after a while, with 30 kilos of the missing drugs —which wasn't too difficult a trick, since he had arranged the hijacking in the first place—and said that was all he could recover. Bacula wasn't upset about the other 20 kilos; Diamond was obviously entitled to them as a commission for returning the 30. Diamond suggested that the remaining drugs be moved to another hotel where they could be under the protection of his gang. For this idea Bacula didn't care much at all, but he was alone in New York and in no position to argue. The move was made, and a Diamond man was assigned to spend the night with the drugs. The next morning he was found with his wrists slashed, and the drugs were gone. Bacula didn't make a nickel out of that trip, and he couldn't even be sure whether Diamond had stolen the drugs from himself, whether the Newmans had stolen them from Diamond, or whether some entirely different gang had made off with them. Elias, of course, suffered nothing from this catastrophe. The Newmans had bought the drugs from him on his usual terms, cash in advance. Only once was Elias ever known to deviate from his cash in advance policy, and his experience that time was enough to convince him never to do it again. In 1929 he sold Big Nose Willie Fleischman, a principal competitor of the Newmans, 50 kilograms on credit. Elias waited patiently for his money for several months before becoming persuaded that Big Nose Willie was giving him the double cross. It may have been a coincidence, but a few days after Elias had reached that conclusion, a band of Corsicans invaded Big Nose Willie's speakeasy on Fifty-second Street and gave him an exceptionally thorough mussing up. Big Nose Willie lived, but he took no more trips to Europe.

5 *America, land of opportunity*

One of Elias's principal objectives when he went into business was to get a firm foothold in the American market. The American market never was nearly so large as the Chinese market, due to the efficient work of the narcotics control officials in the United States, and the clientele was not nearly so genteel, but the profits were enormous. Elias found that he could turn a hundred percent profit merely by selling to American importers in France, and he knew that if he could figure out some way of cutting in on the profits of the retail trade in the United States he could do a great deal better than that. A kilogram of morphine or heroin cost Elias between a hundred and a hundred and twenty-five dollars. American importers paid him between two hundred and twenty and two hundred and fifty dollars a kilogram; when they got the drugs into the United States they would generally adulterate them by fifty percent, making two kilograms out of one, and then were able to sell an adulterated kilogram to a wholesaler for something like five hundred dollars. The wholesaler adulterated the drugs some more, of course, and so did the retailer, so that by the time the drugs reached the addicts, who bought by the ounce or fraction of an ounce, a pure, unadulterated, Eliopoulos kilogram represented two or three thousand dollars gross income. Net profits, of course, were not as sensational as these figures would indicate. All along the line there were business expenses: Paris hotel bills, shipping costs, purchase of adulterants, salaries of minor employees, payoffs to police officers, and so forth, plus a certain amount that always had to be written off because of seizure by the customs or hijacking by rival gangs. Nevertheless the profits were very handsome, and many of the items that figure largely in the budgets of legitimate business—taxes, advertising and publicity, depreciation of plant and machinery, office expenses, and interest on bonded indebtedness—were absent from the calculations of the traffickers.

It was in the fall of 1929 that Elias got his first opportunity to make some real headway in the American trade. That spring, in New York, one Sam Bernstein, a stout, moist man with considerable experience both as a drug trafficker and a bootlegger, went into partnership with two old playmates from his Lower East Side youth, Jake Polakiewitz and Nathan Brooks, with the ostensible purpose of smuggling Scotch malt in from Europe. Bernstein was acquainted with a certain Jacob Bloom, who made his residence in France and knew how business was done there. He was sure Bloom could lead him to some excellent Scotch malt, and proposed that Bloom be made a fourth partner in the enterprise, which Polakiewitz and Brooks agreed to. Presently Bernstein and Polakiewitz sailed for France on the *Mauretania*. They met Bloom in Paris. Bloom was unable to find them any Scotch malt, but he arranged a rendezvous for them with Leonoff-Goldstein, who was acting as Elias's American expert. As a result of this meeting they returned to the United States in August, accompanied by two carefully constructed trunks, in the false bottom of each of which was 25 kilograms of morphine, a considerably more profitable item than Scotch malt. When they had disposed of their merchandise, the partners made definite arrangements to continue in the drug business. Polakiewitz and Bernstein were to return to Europe to purchase the drugs and send them out. The means of shipping was to continue to be double-bottomed trunks, which would be put aboard ship in the name of some passenger. Brooks, known as Nigger Nate because of his carefully cultivated sun-lamp complexion, was to remain in New York. When the trunks were safely aboard ship, he was to be notified by a telegram signed with the name under which the drugs were being shipped, for example, "Aunt Mary arriving Berengaria September 6. George Anderson." Brooks would then meet the *Berengaria* on the appointed day, locate the Anderson trunks on the dock, affix forged customs inspection stamps to them while no one was looking, and have the trunks carted past the barrier. He was entrusted with disposing of the drugs in New York, and with wiring his partners in Paris sufficient funds for more purchases.

When these arrangements had been worked out, Bernstein and Polakiewitz returned to Paris, looked up Leonoff-Goldstein and commenced operations. They were able to send out two or three trunks every month, none of which contained less than 25 kilograms of drugs, and their scheme for getting the trunks past the U.S. Customs proved very successful, particularly once Nigger Nate had made the acquaintance of a customs inspector who felt the civil service pay scale was much too low. In a couple of months the New York end of the business had become much more complex than the Paris end, which was strictly routine, and so Polakiewitz returned home to help Nigger Nate out. In December, 1929, by which time four or five successful shipments had been made, Leonoff-Goldstein told Bernstein that the real suppliers of the drugs were the Eliopoulos brothers—George and Nasso were spending a good deal of time in Paris by now—and that the brothers were very anxious to meet such a successful customer personally. Bernstein was very happy about his arrangements just as they were. He didn't want to meet anyone. Leonoff-Goldstein insisted, however, and Bernstein had to give in.

The meeting Leonoff-Goldstein aranged between Bernstein and Elias, at a café on the Place de la Bastille, justified Bernstein's apprehensions. Elias was charming and hospitable, but what he wanted was precisely what Sam didn't want to give him, a piece of the American profits. The evening was spent in an inconclusive verbal fencing match, and since neither man could afford to antagonize the other, they parted with many protestations of mutual esteem. They also agreed to meet the following day so that Elias could take Sam on a tour of his warehouse, and introduce him to George. At the warehouse, which in addition to several hundred pounds of drugs and quantities of packing cases, also contained a large assortment of clocks, rugs, dried peas and other items suitable for camouflaging contraband, Elias and George renewed their proposals. After pointing out to Sam that the very place in which they were talking was evidence that their facilities for doing business were immense, they suggested that he allow them to handle the shipping of his drugs to the United States. Their motive for making this proposal became quite clear when they added that under such an arrangement they would be able to put some drugs of their own in each shipment, which Sam could sell for them at American prices. Sam replied, as tactfully as possible, that he was well satisfied with the shipping procedures then in force and that, besides, he couldn't do a thing without consulting his partners. George and Elias had to be satisfied for the time being with his assurance that he would think things over. From then on Sam saw the brothers almost every day. They entertained him lavishly, recommended him to a trunk company that specialized in double-bottomed trunks, went out of their way to provide him with all the drugs he wanted, and kept urging him to go into business with them. After three or four weeks of being badgered, Sam, whose ethics were no loftier than anyone else's, finally agreed to let them deliver a shipment their way—provided, of course, that his partners were told nothing about it. He had been sending Nigger Nate a trunk a week ever since he had become acquainted with the Eliopouloses, and he figured that his partners would be sufficiently occupied with the firm's affairs not to notice a little extracurricular activity on his part. This shipment consisted of 100 kilos of heroin, 75 of which had been purchased by Sam and 25 of which he was to sell for the brothers. He watched while it was packed, at the warehouse, into ten cases of statuary, and then sailed for New York, where he was instructed to await a phone call. The greatest precautions had been taken to keep this trip secret from Sam's partners. He left at a time—it was January, 1930—when Bloom was out of Paris; he sailed third class under an assumed name, and he let no one know he was in New York. After sitting by his telephone for a week, he got a call from a mysterious man who refused to identify himself except as being from "the Greeks." He told Sam to take a taxi to Ninth Avenue and Forty-seventh Street, where he would find another taxi parked. He was to enter the other taxi. Sam followed instructions and found inside the second cab a short dark man who silently held out a torn half of a business card, which Sam had presented to Elias in Paris. Sam pulled the other half of the card from his pocket and fitted the two pieces together. The short dark man nodded and pointed to two trunks strapped on the back of the cab. Sam had them transferred to the back of his cab and drove home. The fact that the heroin had been removed from the packing cases and put into trunks impressed Sam. He took it to mean that the Eliopouloses had a headquarters right in New York. As soon as he disposed of the drugs, which didn't take him very long, he slipped back to Paris. He still couldn't see his way clear, though, either to cutting the brothers in or to deserting his partners, and he told Elias so when he saw him, apologizing profusely for his inability to cooperate. Elias shrugged. "Ah, well, *les affaires sont les affaires*," he said blandly, and sold Sam another 50 kilos. Sam sent this lot off in his customary way, on the *Majestic*. For the first time he ran into trouble. The trunk was seized by the U.S. Customs in New York on February 18. Sam was too upset by this unexpected blow to appreciate the humorous aspects of the seizure: The trunk had been shipped in the name of Sir Duncan Orr-Lewis, a distinguished and honorable Englishman, and his lordship's anguish at being connected with a trunkful of heroin would have seemed hilarious under more favorable circumstances. Gamely, Sam tried again. He bought 70 kilos more, and sent them off in two trunks on the *Ile de France*, due in New York March 4. It arrived on that very date, and the Customs promptly seized those trunks, too. Sam began to get the idea. He went to the Eliopouloses and told them that, after mature consideration, he had reached the conclusion that their shipping facilities were better than his. They did not say, "I told you so." They just smiled and clasped his hand.

The *Majestic* and *Ile de France* seizures were the result of unusual prudence and foresight on Elias's part. Among the authorized *courtiers* with whom he had done business in Paris from the very first was a Rumanian named Seja Moses who some of the time claimed to be an Austrian named Rudolph Reiter, and some of the time claimed to be an Afghan citizen born in Beirut named either Seja Moses or Rudolph Reiter. He was a sallow, shifty-looking specimen who during the First World War had been a spy for either the Germans or the French or, more likely still, both. As a *courtier* he was Reiter. Also as a *courtier* he made a deal with Elias whereby he turned over to Elias the supply of blank *bons de toxiques* that had been issued to him and gave his full permission to Elias to forge the name of Reiter on them. In return he was to receive a royalty of one pound sterling a kilogram for all drugs Elias obtained through the forged *bons*. The French narcotics police was pretty inadequate—there were, in fact, only three or four detectives assigned to narcotics duty in the entire country—but it wasn't so inadequate that such egregious goings-on escaped attention indefinitely. One of

the detectives assigned to narcotics work was a certain Inspector Passy of the Sureté, who was extremely well informed about the drug traffic, and who detected the
spuriousness of the Reiter *bons* at an early date. One day
in August, 1929, he set out to find Reiter and demand
an explanation from him. As he was walking down the
street he met Elias accompanied by a sallow shifty-looking
Turkish trafficker who was in Paris to discuss the Smyrna
situation. Passy mistook the Turk for Reiter, and arrested
him, and Elias too. "Two hours later," as Reiter was to
declare bitterly some years afterward, "they were all sitting in a café drinking apéritifs." Passy and Elias had
reached an understanding of considerable mutual advantage. Passy had agreed that, under certain conditions, he
would not molest Elias in any of his business dealings. The
conditions were not onerous: Elias was to guarantee that
no drugs were distributed illegally in France; he was to
pay Passy 5000 francs a month; and, most important of all
to both parties, he was to inform Passy of the activities of
rival traffickers. This last condition not only made it easy
for Elias to keep down competition, but also made it
possible for Passy to compile an impressive record without
working very hard at it. Passy, through a third party, was
to be entitled to all rewards paid for information leading
to the seizure of contraband drugs, but he was to reim-
burse Elias for any expenses incurred in obtaining such
information. It was to this arrangement that Sam was
indebted for the *Majestic* and *Ile de France* seizures.

Elias's victory over Sam was crushing, but for a while it
looked as if it were also strictly Pyrrhic. The *Majestic* and
Ile de France seizures had created consternation in the
breasts of Sam's associates back in New York. They sent
him no money for further purchases, giving the excuse

that, under the circumstances, they had no money to send. Sam's name had been mentioned by the U.S. authorities in connection with the *Majestic* job—Sam, in fact, went to jail for that very shipment some five years later, when the law finally found him—and the general opinion was that lying low was the best course. Polakiewitz silently withdrew from the whole venture, and Nigger Nate was ready to follow him. Polakiewitz's defection, however, revealed the presence of a thitherto silent partner, a certain Louis Adelman, who had been Polakiewitz's financial backer. Adelman was a malevolent little man whose unusual facial development had led his associates to bestow on him the nickname of Fish. He was a white slaver by profession, dealing extensively with South America, and in the course of his career he had picked up a good deal of ready cash, and a vocabulary whose range of obscenity was considered outstanding by all who knew him. Adelman did not propose to go out of business meekly; he had, as he was fond of saying, an investment to protect. Packing $50,000 and a couple of clean shirts into a suitcase, he sailed for France. On May 28 he presented himself to Sam, at the Hotel Belgravia, and announced that he was moving in and taking over. To state that Sam was charmed by either Adelman's personality, or his announcement, would be to tell an untruth. However he was broke, and Adelman had $50,000, so he concealed his feelings as well as he was able, and introduced Adelman to Leonoff-Goldstein. Leonoff-Goldstein was not the man Adelman wanted to meet, however; he wanted to meet the Greeks, but the Greeks, who were happy with Sam, did not want to meet him. Once again Adelman pointed out that he was the fellow with the $50,000. They agreed to see him. Elias did not like Adelman—few people ever did—but he liked the color of his money, and after a certain amount of ceremonial haggling, he agreed to sell him 200 kilos of morphine for $48,000. Adelman promptly paid the money, in cash. Elias said he had only 100 kilos on hand for immediate shipment, and added that it would be better to divide the merchandise into two parts anyhow, so that not so much would be lost in case of seizure by the American customs. The brothers were to take care of the shipping and the delivery in New York. The first shipment was to be sent in three cases of a ten-case consignment of lamps, lamp shades and globes. Each of the three cases would contain eighteen packages of morphine in cubes. When the brothers had completed all the preliminary preparations, they allowed Sam and Adelman to inspect the shipment, and told them that it would arrive in New York some time in July and that they had better hurry back to get it. Sam and Adelman sailed for Quebec on the *Empress of Scotland,* and arrived there July 5. They waited in Quebec until they received a telegram from Paris stating, "Sister arriving Innoku, Black Diamond Line, Hoboken, July 18." They then motored down to New York and took an expectant posture in Sam's apartment on West Seventy-fifth Street.

Meanwhile, in Paris, the traffic had become considerably more complex. During the spring the French government had formed the ill-natured resolution of enforcing its narcotics laws. On June 1 all factories and *courtiers* were given three months' notice to wind up their affairs. On September 1, the government announced, a new license would be issued to anyone who deserved one. Elias and the other traffickers had been prepared for this for some time, and their plans for moving their factories to Turkey were already complete, but even so the actual business of transferring such large scale operations involved a lot of work, and called for friendly relations, while there was still time, with the police. Elias had Adelman's $48,000, and he didn't like Adelman anyway, so as soon as the *Innoku* had left Antwerp, he informed his friend, Inspector Passy, about the shipment, and Passy, in turn, told the American authorities. When the ship got to Hoboken it was promptly overrun by customs men, who had little difficulty locating the drugs. The American government was paying, at the time, $100 a kilogram reward for information leading to seizures, so that Passy came into some ten thousand dollars, enough money to make him feel exceptionally well-disposed toward Elias during this critical period. Adelman's reaction to these developments was not as genial as Passy's, though. Only the thought that another 100 kilos would soon be on their way kept him comparatively calm. October was the month that the second shipment was expected, but October came and went without a word from Paris. Adelman began to badger Sam for action, but Sam, who had been indicted in October for the *Majestic* shipment, was a fugitive from justice and was working full time at remaining one. He told Adelman to go to Paris himself and have it out with the Greeks. In December Adelman took his second trip, accompanied by his wife, Ida. He found Elias polite, but evasive. He had turned over Adelman's second hundred kilos to Leonoff-Goldstein for shipment, he said. Then, just as the shipment was about to be made, Leonoff-Goldstein had been called on urgent business to Harbin, in Manchuria. Adelman, he said, would just have to wait until Leonoff-Goldstein got back from Harbin; it was Leonoff-Goldstein who had misappropriated the drugs, not Elias. Adelman did not find this tale very soothing, but it was the best one he could get, although he tried for two months to get a better one. Finally Elias, with the lordly air of a man who buys a panhandler a meal just to shut him up, gave Adelman five thousand dollars. He made it clear, though, that that was all he would donate. Adelman was sick and tired of Elias and Paris by then, and he had become thoroughly convinced, besides, that the duration of Leonoff-Goldstein's stay in Manchuria depended entirely on the duration of his stay in Paris. He and Ida went home, in March, 1931, muttering about Greeks. He still claims Elias owes him $19,000.

While Adelman had been buying his 200 kilos in the spring of 1930, Sam had privately and surreptitiously made a deal with the brothers for 100 kilos to be sent to him, personally. He had agreed that with this shipment the brothers could send some stuff of their own, if they wanted to, which he would distribute for them in the States. As an extra consideration he was allowed to purchase his 100 kilos for $22,000 instead of $24,000. Sam didn't have $22,000, but, on the sly, he got in touch with Polakiewitz in New York, and had him send the money over. Before leaving Paris with Adelman, Sam pointed out to the brothers that, because of the trouble he was in over the *Majestic* seizure, he would undoubtedly not be able to get back to France for some time. Elias said it didn't matter. He had a man going back and forth across the Atlantic every couple of months, he said, who would act as intermediary. This individual was an athletic-looking Rumanian with close-cropped blond curls whose name was Albert Schwartz. Schwartz was a man of varied experience, having been arrested at least a dozen times on charges ranging from burglary to assault by the time he left Rumania in 1920, before reaching his majority.

Some months after departing his native land he had turned up in Istanbul and had fallen in with Leonoff-Goldstein, who was smuggling diamonds and negotiable securities out of Russia, then in the throes of civil war. Schwartz had worked for Leonoff-Goldstein as a courier, carrying the stuff, via Simplon Express, from Istanbul to the markets in Western Europe. After the Russian vein had been mined out, Schwartz had left Europe to try his luck in Mexico and the United States, where he operated successfully for a while as a confidence man and occasional burglar, and made a number of valuable contacts. In 1929 he found himself unemployed, so he had returned to Europe to look for work. In Paris he ran into his old employer, Leonoff-Goldstein, who recommended him to Elias. Elias saw the value of having on his payroll a man with Schwartz's American connections, and hired him. Schwartz's first assignment for Elias was to accompany another Eliopoulos courier on a smuggling expedition through Mexico to Los Angeles, where certain drugs were to be delivered to one Black Tony, and whatever stolen securities Black Tony may have been able to get his hands on were to be picked up and brought back to Paris for quick and quiet sale there. By the time Schwartz returned from this mission, which was successfully accomplished, Elias was seeing a good deal of Sam, and Schwartz sat in on a number of their conferences. Between conferences he delivered drugs for the brothers to Mexico and the United States, and ran whatever other errands there were on the western side of the Atlantic. This was still his position in the fall of 1930, while Sam was concealing himself from the law. He saw Sam several times during September, October and November, and in the middle of the latter month he wrote

Sam to expect a shipment of 500 kilograms of morphine, manifested as 25 cases of furs, on the S.S. *Alesia* out of Istanbul and due to arrive at the foot of 31st Street, Brooklyn on December 5. Of this shipment, 100 kilograms were the drugs Sam had paid for, and 400 were the property of the Greeks, which Sam was to sell for them. It was when he received the news of the *Alesia* shipment that Sam hustled Adelman off to Paris. To Sam's extreme mortification, however—and to the brothers' as well, this time—word of the shipment had again reached the U.S. Customs. The *Alesia* seizure, some 1100 pounds of pure morphine, still stands as one of the largest single seizures of drugs ever made in this country. It was an important event for another reason, too, for it was the first conclusive evidence that the League of Nations enforcement machinery was finally beginning to operate, and that the narcotics traffic, hitherto solidly united under Elias's leadership, was beginning to become demoralized and torn by internal dissension.

7 *The law foments disorder*

By the time of the *Alesia* seizure the French government had made good its intention of chasing whatever drug traffickers it knew about out of the country. Not unduly alarmed, Elias and his associates had shifted operations to Turkey. The Belgian Paul Mechelaere and the Frenchman L——, Elias's two tame manufacturers, had combined forces to open at Kuskundjuk, a suburb of Istanbul on the Asiatic side of the Bosporus, a factory with a capacity of almost a ton of morphine a month. At the same time a Turkish rogue named Nissim Taranto, together with a group of Mechelaere's former associates, had built the Etkim factory, almost as large, at Eyub, on the Golden Horn. Elias had contributed financial backing to both manufacturers. Shipping facilities from Istanbul were, of course, admirable. Elias and his associates had reason to believe that their merchandise would flow as effortlessly out of Turkey as it had flowed out of France.

They were quite mistaken. The expulsion of the traffickers from France had been more than just a whim of the French government. The League of Nations machinery for the control of the narcotics trade did not have the force of law within the borders of any country until the government of that country passed legislation ratifying it, but it did have behind it the power of publicity. A government which failed to cooperate with the League's efforts to put down the narcotics traffic, sooner or later found itself in the embarrassing position at League meetings of being publicly excoriated for its failure; among the most vehement of the cooperating nations, furthermore, were such influential powers as Great Britain, Germany and the United States. (The United States, although not a League member, was particularly active in the League's narcotics control work.) It was just such a public airing of the French situation that had led to the tightening of the French laws, and had driven the traffic to Istanbul. And the Turkish government's fear that it would be roughly handled in Geneva before long, made the life of the traffickers in Istanbul much less easy than they had expected it to be.

In addition, several of the provisions of the League's control machinery were carefully calculated to demoralize the traffic from within. The most important of these was the posting of rewards for information leading to the seizure of contraband narcotics. These rewards were not so substantial in themselves as to offer a serious financial temptation to the traffickers; the League's action appealed to their cupidity in a much more subtle way, for it provided a ready-made and efficient apparatus for getting rid of competitors. The first man to succumb to the lure of the League's reward system was a downy-cheeked, pop-eyed Turk named Eli Abou Isaac, whom Taranto had hired as the shipping expediter for the Etkim factory. Isaac, who generally gallicized his name into Elie Abouissac, had made a career of being on confidential terms with Turkish customs officials and forwarding companies, and Taranto relied upon him to manage the business of getting the drugs safely out of Turkey; the arrangement between them was that Abouissac was to receive a two-pound-sterling royalty for each kilogram of drugs that passed through his hands. Out of this he was to pay his own expenses, including the wages of anyone he hired to help him. As his first two employees he carefully chose a pair of old associates of his, a questionable Italian named Lorenzetti, and a Greek named Stamatis Astras who had the reputation of being the most consummate villain in Eastern Europe, a pretty large order. Abouissac, Lorenzetti and Astras were not in the least interested in expediting Taranto's shipments for such starvation wages as two pounds a kilogram, which only would have amounted to a thousand pounds a month for the three of them. They prepared and put into effect an uncouth, but very successful, system of blackmail. Abouissac and Lorenzetti remained in Istanbul, ostensibly as Taranto's employees, and made it their business to become informed of all the activities not only of their employer but also of the Kuskundjuk people. Astras opened an office in Paris and forthrightly declared himself an "accredited informant of the League of Nations." Relaying to the League the information he received from his partners in Turkey, he managed to have several shipments seized in various parts of the globe—and, of course, collected the rewards. Abouissac then revealed to the Istanbul manufacturers that he had been the fellow responsible for the seizures, and told them that from now on he wanted substantial amounts of drugs donated to him so that he would not be forced to do any further talking. When the manufacturers demurred, he introduced them to another member of his staff, an Al

Capone-type Corsican named Carbone who had a large reputation in the Levant as a wicked man with a knife. The drugs Abouissac extorted, he sent to Astras on the person of a Bulgarian Wagon-Lits porter. Astras distributed them, showing a special fondness for dispatching them into Egypt via Marseille, where Carbone owned a brothel and was a local power. Astras's position as "accredited informant" made him safe from even such a relentless police force as the Egyptian Central Narcotics Intelligence Bureau; the information he gave out about other traffickers was too valuable, and his actions disrupted the traffic too thoroughly, for any policeman to want to put him behind bars.

And so by the end of 1930, the traffic, which Elias had so painstakingly welded into a monolithic unit, had fallen into pieces again, and although many of the pieces remained in his hands, even more had slipped out of them. The perfidy of the Abouissac-Lorenzetti-Astras partnership had transformed the traffic into a maelstrom of treachery and malice. Traffickers who had been on the most cordial terms for years now betrayed one another to the police. The seizure of the 500 kilos of morphine on the *Alesia* was the result of this new state of affairs. J——, the veteran French smuggler who had helped Elias get started in the business, deserted the standard, believing that Astras's was the rising star. In return, Elias, of course, took every opportunity of discommoding Astras and J——, often taking immense pains in the process. At the close of one long expensive trip Elias took to Istanbul to study the movements and technique of Astras's partners, he learned that J—— and Carbone were about to board a train for Paris, with 20 kilos of drugs. He went to the railroad station to see if he could make peace with J——. As he was remonstrating with his former associate, Carbone arrived, whipped out his revolver, and crowned Elias with the butt end of it. He and J—— then hopped aboard the train, which was pulling out. When Elias's skull stopped throbbing, he promptly wired the Paris authorities to intercept the shipment. J—— was not to be caught that easily, though. Knowing what the result of Carbone's fervor would be, he ditched the drugs, and presented a perfect picture of outraged innocence to the gendarmes. After this episode reconciliation became entirely out of the question.

In an atmosphere this rancorous, Elias's personal position, founded on his reputation as an eminent and respectable capitalist, was bound to become precarious; in the spring of 1931, it was, as a matter of fact, seriously jeopardized by another former intimate, David Gourievidis, the man who had first introduced him to the traffic. Elias and Gourievidis had been eyeing one another distrustfully for some time. Gourievidis suspected that Elias had been responsible for the seizure of certain Chinese shipments of his. Elias suspected that Gourievidis had been responsible for the seizure of certain Chinese shipments of *his*. Both suspicions were undoubtedly well founded, but the two men had tactfully remained on speaking terms. In April, 1931, Gourievidis arrived in Paris and tried to look Elias up. Elias was not in town. The transfer of operations to Turkey had led him to spend a good deal of time in Eastern Europe, and he had left the management of the decreasingly important Parisian end of the business to his two younger brothers, George, who had moved in from Rumania a year before and had set up a "bank" as a front for the brothers' activities, and Athanasios, or Nasso, who divided his time between Paris and Athens. Gourievidis found Nasso in, and moved into his apartment for a few days' stay. Compared with the sophisticated Elias, Nasso was a crude, undiplomatic fellow. It wasn't long before he and Gourievidis were engaging in mutual recriminations, and it wasn't much longer before Nasso threatened blows. Gourievidis, an unathletic type, departed hurriedly, but he soon returned, escorted by Carbone, and dared Nasso to repeat what he had just said. Nasso responded by bellowing, "Help! Police!" Carbone did not care to improve further his already extensive acquaintance with the gendarmerie —although some years later, as a participant in the Stavisky scandal, he was to do just that. He made a quick getaway. Gourievidis, however, stood his ground. When the police arrived Nasso accused Gourievidis of attempted robbery. Both characters were hauled off to the nearest precinct and questioned. Gourievidis cleared himself of the charge without difficulty; he didn't even carry a gun, since that was Carbone's department. He was so enraged by Nasso's perfidy, though, that he lost control of his tongue and suddenly found himself accusing the Eliopoulos brothers of being narcotics traffickers.

Gourievidis's charges, although he withdrew them as soon as he recaptured his temper, and the French authorities were unable to act upon them anyway for lack of substantiation, created a private sensation among the narcotics police of several countries. They were particularly gratifying to a taciturn Harvard graduate named Charles B. Dyar who ever since 1927 had been Treasury attaché to the American Embassy in Paris, with the specific duty of gathering information about the narcotics traffic. Dyar was an unobtrusive but efficient detective who had managed to gain entrée to circles in which many of the traffickers moved; intelligence which he had acquired had led to several important seizures of contraband drugs by the United States Customs. He had been personally persuaded for some time that Elias was the key figure in the traffic, but he had been unable to produce any evidence conclusive enough to permit him to assail a man of his standing, and he had received little help from the French authorities, largely because the only Sureté inspector who knew anything about narcotics was on Elias's payroll. Dyar's interest in the Gourievidis story was shared by a number of other energetic policemen, among them Inspector Werner Thomas, the astute narcotics expert of the Berlin police, and, of course, Russell Pasha. One of the most useful provisions of the League's convention for the international control of narcotics had been the pooling of information; policemen from a dozen countries had been in close touch with one another for several years. Gourievidis's unbridled tongue was an inspiration to them all.

The first result of Gourievidis's outburst was that the governments of several countries, including the United States, Great Britain and Germany, strongly, if unofficially, urged the French government to expel the Eliopoulos brothers from France as undesirable aliens. These representations were so reasonable that Elias's friend in the Sureté was unable to prevent an order of expulsion from being issued, in May, against all three. Nasso had slipped back to Athens immediately after he had stirred up this hornet's nest, and he was happy to remain there, but for George and Elias the order of expulsion was a calamity. Elias was aware that abandoning France was the only prudent thing to do, since by now his social standing there was irremediably tarnished, but the expulsion involved a great deal of painful business reorganization, and caused him acute personal pangs as well. He had been living in Paris since 1927, and by 1931 he had built up a convivial circle of influential acquaintances; he had established a luxurious residence at 88 Rue Michel-Ange, a stylish address; and he had installed there an agreeable young woman to whom he paid 5000 francs a month to keep his home fires burning. George's problem was even more heart-rending. He had neither Elias's passion for business nor Nasso's tough-minded contempt for public opinion; he was a bumbling fellow whose major interests in life were bridge, cocktails and handsome matrons. He had been in Paris only a year and a half and he had found there, for the first time in his life, ample facilities for gratifying these tastes. Elias wanted George to remain, too. Not only did he like to see his younger brother happy, but he did need a representative in Paris. George pulled every wire that he or Elias could lay a hand on; a prominent Greek diplomat was induced to intervene in his behalf, and several prominent French citizens spoke up for him. He succeeded in having the order stayed until September, but then he had to leave. One of the most telling points against him was that his "bank" on the Place de la Madeleine employed an office staff of two, and that he himself seldom put in more than a couple of hours a week there. Elias would have been better pleased with his brother if these absences from the bank had been for the purpose of attending to the narcotics business. They were, however, largely devoted to indulging his sybaritic whims. On at least two occasions valuable consignments of narcotics were hijacked because George, who had been assigned to keep an eye on things, had gone to a cocktail party instead.

Meanwhile Dyar had instituted researches into Elias's financial position. Since Elias had bank accounts in his name in London, Paris, Berlin, Athens and Berne, and there was no telling how many accounts he had in dummy names or how many well-filled safe deposit boxes he had strewn about, this was quite a project. After several months however, Dyar did manage to come up with one number which he found sufficiently illuminating: Between June, 1930, and July, 1931, Elias had received by telegraph through the American Express Company from Tientsin alone, 150,000 pounds sterling, or $750,000. This was gross income, of course, not net profit, but it seemed a fairly large sum nevertheless, representing, as it did, upward of 5000 kilograms (five tons) of morphine or heroin. The remitter of this money, in all cases, was John D. Voyatzis, the "coffee and tobacco importer," who had not only been Elias's first customer but his best one. Business arrangements between Elias and Voyatzis had been worked out with a precision that might have served as a model for dealers in less dubious commodities. For one thing, Elias and Voyatzis had, at the very beginning of their association, provided for safe and frequent communication between them by devising a code, based on the Universal Trade Code, a commercial cipher in general use. The Universal Trade Code, like all other commercial codes, is designed to save businessmen money. For that purpose it reduces almost every word or phrase that a businessman finds occasion to use to a group of five letters, and a corresponding group of five digits, ranging from 00000 to 99999. All the words and phrases that the Universal Trade Code people could think up are exhausted between 00000 and 74999, including "strenuous measures necessary for," "Banco de Chile," "2%16," "peanut oil," "f.o.b. Port Said," "referring to my letter 15th inst.," "below zero centigrade," "bayerische Hypotheken und Wechselbank," "how are labor conditions at," "Union Steamship Co. of New Zealand," and "torpedoed." That leaves 25,000 extra groups for the users of the code to employ for any especially esoteric words or phrases they might need. The Eliopoulos version of the Universal Trade Code simply involved transposing the middle digit in each group to the front of the group. In the original code, for example, "sold" is 58853. If Elias wanted to send that word to Voyatzis, which he frequently did, he would take the middle 8 and put it in front of the group, making it 85853. He would then look up no. 85853 in the code book, and discover that the letter group corresponding to it was XIQWD, and that was what he sent in his wire. Voyatzis, receiving the wire, looked up XIQWD, and discovered it corresponded to 85853. He would then put the 8 back in the middle, look up 58853 in the book, and find it meant "sold." Anyone who realized this private code was based on the Universal Trade Code would have no trouble at all untangling the traffickers' telegrams, but without the Universal Trade Code book the telegrams were perfectly inscrutable. Elias and Voyatzis also made good use of the extra numbers from 75000 to 99999. 75000, meant "Elias"; 75001 meant "Nasso," and there were provisions made for such other names as "George," "John D.," "Gourievidis," and dozens of others. There were also special groups assigned for all the varieties of drugs, for the chemicals necessary to convert opium into drugs, for the machinery necessary for the same process, for all sorts of containers, for a number of steamship lines not appearing in the original code, and for routes of shipment. An impressive list of commodities in the guise of which drugs were shipped, appeared in the code: vaseline, polishing paste, bathing salts, pois verts ronds, haricots blancs, nouilles, jambon en conserve, crème de riz, eau de cologne, among others. And in addition there were general phrases of particular import to the traffic, such as "don't worry, things are not so dangerous," "the same for George," "am afraid that goods are supervised, try rescue in Shanghai," "wire to address of Elias," "send me the following fictitious telegram by code," and "we are supervised, are afraid of personal mishap." Elias not only had carefully provided for the security of his communications in transit, but he had also set up a series of well-manned receiving and transmitting posts all over Europe. There was a Paris post with the telegraphic address of Govolfer; an Athens post, Simza, generally manned by Nasso, since it was a receiving station for large sums of money; and an Istanbul post, Kosta, in the name of Kosta Belokas, Elias's Middle Eastern expert. When things had deteriorated in France, Elias sent one of his principal lieutenants, Seja Moses—who had been Rudolph Reiter when he had been a licensed drug broker in Paris—to open a clearing house for all messages in Berlin, with the telegraphic address of

Atsok—Kosta backwards. Voyatzis in Tientsin received wires addressed to Sfinx.

It was immediately after the expulsion order was issued in Paris that Elias sent Moses to Berlin to set up Atsok. Elias had resolved to maintain headquarters in Western Europe, first because the amount of available shipping there was much greater than in the Near East, and second to be as far away as possible from the intolerable situation in Istanbul. He chose Germany as his base of operations, despite the efficiency of the German police, for a number of reasons: Germany was full of good alkaloid chemists and manufacturing facilities; one of its two great shipping centers, Hamburg, was a free port, and because commerce in free ports was virtually unrestricted, they were always favored by the traffickers (Trieste was another port in heavy use); furthermore the German authorities did not have the extensive personal acquaintance that the French had with the traffickers, an acquaintance that dated back to the days when the traffic was legal. En route from Paris to Berlin, Moses was commissioned by Elias to secure some drugs for Voyatzis and to arrange to have them sent to China in such a way that Abouissac would have no inkling of the shipment. This errand involved Moses's making the journey by way of Istanbul. Moses, a slight swarthy man, traveled in the company of his mistress, Frau Ethelind Gottlieb, a blonde lady of operatic proportions. Herr Emil Gottlieb, her husband, went along too. In Istanbul Moses looked up Kosta Belokas, Elias's representative there. So all-seeing was Abouissac's eye that it took Kosta three weeks and monumental circumspection to get hold of a mere 81 kilos of morphine. It would have been impossible to maintain this precious security if the drugs had been shipped to China directly out of Istanbul, so Kosta and

Moses worked out a much more elaborate scheme. Kosta was to take the drugs, personally, by sea to Venice. In Venice they would be repacked and shipped by rail through the Brenner Pass to Innsbruck. In Innsbruck they would be stored in a warehouse until Emil Gottlieb picked them up and carried them across the German border. Once in Germany they were to be taken to Hamburg and turned over to a merchant named Karl Frank who had storage and shipping facilities there. He would send them to China at the first opportunity. Kosta gave Moses 1500 Turkish pounds to cement the arrangements in Venice and Innsbruck. Moses and Ethelind then left Istanbul, leaving behind Emil and three trunks of old clothes belonging to Moses and the Gottliebs. The trunks had false bottoms. Toward the end of May Moses and Ethelind got to Berlin, and were able to wire Kosta in Istanbul, Simza in Athens (where Elias was) and Govolfer in Paris (where George was) that all arrangements had been made. He and Ethelind then began looking for an apartment. They found one before many days had passed, and on the day they moved into it, Ethelind purchased a copy of the Universal Trade Code and registered Atsok as her telegraphic address. At about this time Kosta sailed for Venice with the 81 kilos, and, when he arrived, had the drugs trans-shipped according to plan. He then returned to Istanbul and told Emil, who was waiting with the three trunks, that the time to move on to Berlin had come. Emil left, taking a leisurely overland route. On June 27 he stopped for the night in Innsbruck, leaving his trunks, unlocked, in the check room of the railway station. As he slept peacefully in his hotel, a mysterious man induced the check room attendant to allow him to stow several bulky parcels in the false bottoms of two of the trunks. Gottlieb left the following morning, and on June 29 Moses was able to wire Govolfer from Berlin, "Trunks received good order," and Kosta, "Friend arrived good condition." Moses took the trunks to Frank in Hamburg, who put them in his warehouse, pending the departure for Tientsin of an appropriate ship. It wasn't until July 30 that Moses was able to wire Sfinx, "Shipping Hamburg August 12 81 kilos in trunks." The ship that Frank put the drugs on was the *S. S. Havelland.* Two years before, with no trouble at all, a small shipment like that could have been aboard ship at Le Havre three days after it had been purchased by Elias from a factory in a suburb of Paris.

About a week after the *Havelland* sailed, Moses traveled to Lausanne to collect his commission, 10,000 francs, from Elias, and to hold a series of business conferences with him. Ever since spring Elias had been working feverishly on German arrangements that would offset his loss of France as a headquarters, and untangle him from the impossible Turkish situation. These plans involved setting up a narcotics factory at Wandsbeck, and shipping the goods out through the facilities afforded by Karl Frank. Elias had spent a good deal of time effecting a reconciliation with Gourievidis, and it was Gourievidis who had lined up Frank, an old friend from the underworld of tsarist St. Petersburg. While Moses and Elias were discussing these interesting matters, Elias received a plea for funds from the manufactures in Turkey; the Turkish Government had finally succumbed to international pressure, and had ordered the Etkim and Kuskundjuk factories to close down. The manufacturers were planning to move to Bulgaria, but they needed money. Elias wanted no further truck with them, however. The only effect on him of their plea was to make him speed up the Wandsbeck plans. Moses left Lausanne with instructions to purchase in Berlin certain machinery for the conversion of opium into alkaloids. Elias and his mistress, traveling under the name of M. and Mme. Stavridis, then went on to London where Elias wanted to have words with George, who had gone there after being expelled from France. Meanwhile an alternative to the Wandsbeck scheme was being brought to a head in Athens by Nasso. This was to establish a narcotics factory on the high seas, where no national police force would be able to touch it, and it was with this in mind, late in September, Nasso acquired the ownership of the steamship *Anthemis*, of Greek registry. The difficulties and expenses of operating and supplying a floating factory were obviously enormous, and so Elias saved this idea for a dire emergency. Such an emergency arose, soon enough, but it arose so rapidly that Elias was in jail before he could even say "S. S. *Anthemis*."

Elias passed the month of October in London with George, and Moses passed it in Berlin, expediting the Wandsbeck plan and exchanging increasingly fretful telegrams with Sfinx in Tientsin. Voyatzis had not received the *Havelland* shipment and wanted to know where it was; Moses kept insisting that it had been sent out in good order, and demanding the money for it. It wasn't until November 1 that Voyatzis discovered that on September 23 the *Havelland* shipment had been seized at Tientsin by the Chinese Maritime Customs. Elias was in Berlin, on his way back to Athens, when this news came. He wired Sfinx, "Feeling morally broken. Afraid of much larger further catastrophe. Continue remittances to Athens according to instructions of Nasso." This last sentence referred to money for other consignments which Voyatzis apparently was holding up in alarm. Then, after wringing his hands for a couple of days, Elias went on to Athens. A month passed, and still no money came from Tientsin. The first week in December Elias again wired Sfinx, "Telegraph immediate full explanation why you do not remit our money, my blood." This last pathetic plea must have touched Voyatzis's heart, for a couple of weeks later he sent the money. Elias never did find out where the tip that led to the *Havelland* seizure came from, but his best guess, which he kept strictly to himself, was that Gourievidis had something to do with it.

9 *Little Augie's unprofitable journey*

Meanwhile the events that were to lead to Elias's arrest and downfall had been preparing in a wholly unsuspected quarter. When the S.S. *Europa* sailed from New York on May 2, 1931, its first class passenger list included, among others, the names of Adolph Ochs and valet; Mr. S. R. Guggenheim and manservants; Barbara Hutton; Ernest T. Weir; Irving Thalberg and Mrs. Thalberg, and maid, infant and governess. It also included the name of A. Delles. It probably would have pained members of the former, distinguished group—particularly Mr. Guggenheim's manservants and infant Thalberg's governess—if they had known that their shipmate Delles was none other than August Del Gracio, better known as Augie the Wop, and best known as Little Augie—or, as the name appeared in Elias's papers, "Little Oggi." Augie was a short feline thirty-eight-year-old product of the Lower East Side of New York. Between 1910 and 1920 he had served a strenuous criminal apprenticeship that had involved eleven arrests on a wide variety of charges, including assault, grand larceny, homicide, burglary, illegal possession of firearms and peddling narcotics. By 1920 he had graduated from

the exposed position of hoodlum-of-all-work into more rar-
efied strata of the underworld, and although he had been
suspected of all sorts of misdeeds since then, he had never
been caught at any of them. With success he had developed an urbane manner, an extensive vocabulary, a stylish taste in clothes and a predilection for fingering long eb-
ony cigarette holders and tall bosomy blondes in public,
and for smoking an occasional pipe of opium in private.
He had bought six apartment houses in his native quarter,
Chrystie Street, and a prosperous service station on the
Boston Post Road in the Bronx. As a local power he drew
revenues from nearly every bookmaking establishment,
floating crap game, numbers enterprise and massage parlor in his neighborhood, but these represented, merely, the
normal tribute paid any feudal lord. His wealth and influence derived primarily from smuggling narcotics, a
trade of which he had become the most eminent practitioner in the United States. Among his personal effects
when he traveled to Europe was usually three or four hundred thousand dollars in cash. When Mechelaere and
L—— set up the Kuskundjuk factory, Augie financed the
enterprise to the extent of $75,000, which left him in a
position to secure drugs in almost unlimited quantities once
the factory was in operation. He and Elias had never met,
but their paths had necessarily crossed in the course of the
intricate transactions in which they both engaged, and
they had developed feelings of mutual admiration and respect. Although, by the time of his 1931 trip, the United
States government was morally certain that Augie was in
the drug business, it had not been able to obtain facts to
prove it, and it hesitated to refuse him a passport, since
catching him in the act of smuggling drugs would be impossible if he were not permitted to go to Europe and

smuggle them. This policy appeared to be a good risk. By 1931 the exchange of information among the various national narcotics police forces had reached a high degree of effectiveness, and the American authorities felt certain that Augie's activities would be sharply observed no matter how long he was absent from their jurisdiction.

Augie spent a pleasant week at the Hotel Claridge in Paris, sipping champagne and renewing old acquaintances, and then proceeded to Istanbul to confer with the Kuskundjuk people. He was several weeks in Turkey, arranging for a number of large shipments to be sent in various guises and by various routes, and then returned to Paris to await the arrival of the merchandise in Western Europe. One of the consignments he had paid for, and was expecting, was 250 kilograms of morphine in cubes, which Mechelaere had promised to pack in several cases of replacement parts for grease racks, and forward to Karl Frank in Hamburg, who would ship them on to the United States. Augie had every reason, as the owner of a service station, to buy replacement parts for grease racks. So thoroughly was Mechelaere infected, however, by the prevailing atmosphere of treachery, that he could not bear to deal honestly with even such a good customer as Augie. He forwarded the morphine cubes to Hamburg well in advance of the date Augie expected them there, and instead of informing Frank that they were Augie's property, he simply instructed him to extract the morphine from the cases, forward the cases to the United States, and find a buyer for the morphine. Frank found nothing unconventional about these instructions; he was delighted, in fact, to have so large a piece of business turned his way. The plot would have worked perfectly, with Augie not being able to guess where, en route, the drugs were pilfered, if Mechelaere had only told Frank that they were Augie's property. His failure to do this had consequences of the most lamentable kind for everyone, since Frank, searching for a buyer, consulted his chum Gourievidis, and Gourievidis immediately suggested that the morphine be sold to Augie. Gourievidis traveled to Paris, called upon Augie, and told him that Karl Frank in Hamburg was offering 250 kilos of morphine cubes for sale. 250-kilo consignments of morphine cubes, even in those days, were not so common that two of them were likely to turn up in the same warehouse at the same time. Augie was pretty certain that the drugs Gourievidis was talking about were his, and the idea of being asked to buy his own property did not appeal to him. He was too used to this sort of thing to reveal his emotions, though; he merely expressed polite interest in the drugs, asked time to consider, and then, when Gourievidis was out of range, took off for Istanbul like a startled fawn to have a talk with Mechelaere. This was the early part of November.

Mechelaere was just as imperturbable a fellow as Augie. When Augie demanded an explanation of him, he had no trouble giving one: The consignment at Frank's wasn't Augie's at all, but one just like it; Augie's had not yet been sent out. Augie, of course, didn't believe this story, but he couldn't get Mechelaere to change it. And so he looked up Abouissac, the master of the double cross, with the idea that this gentleman's fertile imagination could assist him. He also had several heart-to-heart talks with Kosta Belokas, who assured him that Elias frowned on this sort of thing, and would be glad to use his influence to foil Mechelaere. Then, convinced that he could settle the matter much more expeditiously in Germany than he could in Turkey, Augie made plans to depart. Abouissac agreed to take the trip to Hamburg with him, and Kosta gave him the mystic word Atsok, and told him to call upon Moses in Berlin for whatever help he needed. Augie and Abouissac booked reservations on the Simplon Express for November 28. Augie had been kept under continuous surveillance since his arrival in Europe, though, and so, when the Simplon Express pulled into Berlin's suburbs on November 30, it was boarded by Inspector Thomas's men, who quickly learned from the conductor what compartment Augie and Abouissac occupied, burst in on them, and took them into custody.

Augie was studying some business papers when the constabulary arrived. Unexpected as their appearance was, his customary coolness did not desert him. He calmly folded the documents into a newspaper that lay beside him, casually tossed the newspaper onto the baggage rack above his head, rose, and declared himself ready to accompany his captors. Unfortunately for Augie, the policemen were cool customers too. With a nonchalance that matched his own, they took the paper down from the rack and carried it off together with their prisoner. The documents that Augie had concealed in the newspaper provided interesting reading for Inspector Thomas. There were several letters to Augie from Mechelaere that indiscreetly revealed that Karl Frank in Hamburg was in possession of 250 kilos of morphine cubes, and not many hours had passed before the Hamburg authorities had Frank, several of his colleagues, and the morphine safely in hand. There was also a mysterious piece of paper that bore no other writing than the word Atsok in block letters. The meaning of Atsok did not baffle Inspector Thomas for long. By the following day Moses was behind bars, and all his business records and correspondence were being examined by the Berlin police. Not much could be made of Moses's correspondence, since it consisted almost entirely of coded telegrams, and the code was impossible to break without a key. Thomas was gratified to discover, however, that Moses had also kept a diary and an expense book, and these two items were sufficiently explicit to reveal that Moses was employed by the Eliopoulos brothers, at 1000 marks a month, plus commissions, and also to implicate Gourievidis, Kosta Belokas, and a number of other less sinister figures. Thomas promptly put out an alarm for the Eliopoulos brothers, Gourievidis and whatever other members of the organization might venture into Germany, and saw to it that the French, British, American and all other interested governments were informed in full detail of what had happened. Augie, Moses, Frank and the others, meanwhile, indicated no desire to be communicative, and it looked as if making a case against everyone but Frank would be a long and difficult business. While evidence was being accumulated, the prisoners waited in the Hamburg jail. On December 28 the S.S. *Ceres* put into Hamburg, out of Istanbul. In its hold was a shipment, manifested as gum tragacanth and consigned to Frank. The Hamburg authorities could not very well avoid inspecting this cargo, which turned out to be 1513 kilograms of raw opium, which Augie had purchased from Turkish growers. When he received word of the *Ceres* seizure in his cell, Augie quivered, but still refused to talk. In January, 1932, Gourievidis unwisely set foot on German soil, and was promptly sent to join his colleagues in the Hamburg jail. In the same month the British found Elias in London and began to keep a careful eye on him. He remained there until the beginning of March, when he booked passage across the channel to Rotterdam. The

British police promptly notified their Dutch counterparts, who took up the surveillance as Elias stepped ashore. He went to the railway station and bought a ticket to Lausanne, via Germany. The Dutch police wired the Germans about this. On March 8, German police stepped aboard the Rheingold Express at Mannheim, and a few hours later the Hamburg jail received another boarder.

¹⁰ *Crime seems to have paid*

The expulsion of the Eliopoulos brothers from France, followed by the *Havelland* seizure, followed by the arrests in Hamburg and Berlin, gave John Voyatzis in Tientsin cause to reflect. He was a man in his late fifties; he had spent twenty-five happy years in Tientsin, and had acquired a fortune. He concluded that the time had come for him to abandon the strife and turmoil of the market place, and quietly return to the mountains of his native Greece, there to pass his declining years in the bosom of his family. On February 3, 1932, he sailed from Tientsin on the *S.S. Fulda,* bound for Port Said. International cooperation was at a high pitch all over the place by this time. The British authorities in Tientsin notified Russell Pasha in Egypt of Voyatzis's movements, and so when Voyatzis landed in Port Said on March 6, he was immediately put under surveillance by the Egyptian police. Voyatzis's first acts were to book passage on a ship sailing March 18 from Alexandria to the Piraeus, and to send his heavy baggage direct from Port Said to Alexandria. He himself then proceeded to Cairo where he spent a gay week and a half playing the stock market. He did not make connections with any suspicious persons during that time. The day before his ship was to sail, Russell Pasha had the baggage searched in Alexandria. It yielded a fruity prize: an address book and a code book. The address book contained the name and address of just about every important trafficker in Europe. The code book contained a complete key to Elias's code, which, when it was relayed to the German police, immediately made Seja Moses's correspondence file perfectly intelligible, and revealed all the details of the *Havelland* affair. When Voyatzis went to his stateroom on the 18th, and found that his baggage had been ransacked, he was fearfully annoyed, but he would have swallowed his emotions had not the passenger in the next cabin commenced cursing the Egyptian police in tones that could be heard right through the bulkhead. Voyatzis looked in his neighbor's door and asked him what the matter was. The neighbor said his baggage had been ruthlessly searched in Alexandria, some of his valuables had been stolen, and that the Egyptian authorities should all be consigned to hell's most abysmal pit. Before he knew what he was saying Voyatzis told the man that the very same thing had happened to him. By the time the voyage to the Piraeus was over Voyatzis and his neighbor were confidential friends, and Voyatzis had talked at length of the Chinese narcotics traffic. Since his confidant was one of Russell Pasha's men, a *bimbashi*, or major, in the Egyptian police, this was indiscreet of Voyatzis. The only result of the indiscretion, though, was to amplify Russell Pasha's knowledge of the traffic. No charges could be found that would convict Voyatzis. He retired to the mountains, as he had planned, and although Marc, as the *bimbashi* was called, visited him there frequently, no information sufficient to send him to jail was ever forthcoming.

The address book and the code book, together with Voyatzis's loose talk, the now decipherable contents of Moses's files, and statements that Moses and Gourievidis finally decided to make to the Hamburg authorities, tied up almost all the loose ends of the international narcotics traffic as it had been conducted since 1927. "The Drug Barons of Europe," as Russell Pasha was to call the Eliopoulos brothers in his report to the League of Nations for the year of 1932, had lost their barony. Elias's fall did not, of course, signify that the narcotics traffic had been abolished, but it did represent the end of its palmiest, or ton-lot, era. Never since then has the traffic reached proportions remotely equivalent to those it enjoyed under Elias's leadership, and it probably never will, for international controls, first under the League and now under the United Nations, have become increasingly effective. The success of the police in abating the traffic has not been matched by equal success in punishing traffickers, however. Elias and his brothers and associates were severely inconvenienced by the events of 1931 and 1932, but most of them eluded the full measure of retribution with extreme agility. The Hamburg case dragged on for years. The court calendar was crowded, it was difficult to develop any very conclusive evidence connecting Elias with the Hamburg seizure, and, most important, political conditions in Germany in 1932 made a number of problems seem more important than the narcotics traffic to policemen, judges and other public officials. All the prisoners were released on bail by the end of April, after they had been questioned at length, and Elias, Gourievidis and Moses were permitted to leave the country almost immediately afterwards. Augie hung around Hamburg for several months, adhering to a rigid daily schedule that involved rising at three in the afternoon, and patronizing the local cafés, dance halls, and other native habitats of tall bosomy blondes every night until sunrise. In December, by which time German officials were even less concerned with narcotics than they had been in April, he was given permission to return home. Karl Frank, having no passport at all, just sat around and waited. He was finally tried in November, 1934, was convicted and sentenced to nine months in prison. No charges ever had been made against Abouissac, first because it was impossible to demonstrate that he was involved with the Hamburg morphine at all, and second because of the high hopes cherished by the police that he would turn informer. He withdrew to the Levant early in 1932. For the next two or three years he was in intermittent communication with United States Narcotics Bureau agents in Europe, promising to tell all about Augie and Elias, but the price he asked for this information was more than the Treasury could stand, and so his revelations never were made. The charges against Moses were dropped in return for a series of confessions he made. His connection with the Hamburg morphine was also pretty tenuous. When Gourievidis left Germany he went to China, where his brothers were still active in the narcotics business. He returned to Europe from time to time, however, and maintained contact with Elias, who had holed up in Athens, and was trying to restore his reputation as a respectable citizen. Late in 1935 Elias persuaded Gourievidis that the Germans were no longer interested in the whole business, and that he should go to Hamburg, stand trial, be acquitted, and thus remove the stain from his name. Elias, of course, was sim-

ply making a test run with Gourievidis; he wanted to find
out just how serious the Germans still were, feeling that if
acquittal seemed probable, it would be worth while to be
tried himself. He found out; Gourievidis was sentenced to
two years in prison and fined ten thousand marks. In
1938 the Hamburg authorities wrote Elias in Athens, in-
viting him to deliver himself up. He wrote a courteous
letter in reply, stating that the Greek government's regulations about taking money out of the country made it
impossible for him to afford the expense of a trip to Germany, and he would therefore, regretfully, have to decline the kind invitation.

Augie remained in New York, under the Narcotics Bureau's watchful eye, from 1933 to 1936. Because of the
Ceres and Hamburg seizures, and his long absence, he
found business had fallen off drastically, and he began
more and more to think about how to get back to Europe
and resume his activities. Late in 1936 he finally took out
a passport, telling the State Department that his intention was to go back to Hamburg, stand trial, and recover
the ten-thousand-mark bail he had left there. The State
Department had been alerted by the Narcotics Bureau
for just such an emergency, and was prepared to give
Augie a passport good only for Germany and only for
three months. Through a clerical error, however, it was
made good for France also, and so Augie calmly walked off
the S.S. *President Harding* at Le Havre on October 22,
1936, and disappeared. Inspector Thomas had no intention of letting him get away with that. The Germans immediately asked the French to pick him up and send him
to Germany, and the Americans added some unofficial
pressure in the same cause. On October 31 Augie was
arrested in Paris. On December 29, his extradition was

approved, and he was sent to Hamburg. He was tried in February 1937, and sentenced to two years in prison and ten thousand marks fine. He served until November, 1938—six months, representing the time he had been confined before being convicted, were taken off the sentence —and then was unceremoniously sent back to New York, with his passport in the custody of the captain of the ship that carried him.

As soon as Elias had been released on bail in the spring of 1932, he had returned to Athens, with the intention of staying there for good. His purpose was to reestablish the honor of his family name. Since he was considerably richer than he had been when he had left Athens five years before, this project did not seem to him to present many obstacles. One of the first steps he took in his carefully planned campaign of self-reclamation was to tell *Bimbashi* Marc, who had remained in Greece at Russell Pasha's order, that he was ready to make a statement about his past. His motive in making this offer was not only to create an impression by behaving in a frank and manly manner, but also to whitewash George. George was in and out of Athens, acting sullen, and giving his big brother a hard time; he still wanted to live in Paris, and Elias hoped that a statement denying that George was involved in any part of the traffic would induce the French authorities to permit him to return. Russell Pasha regarded Elias's proposed confession as so important, that he induced the U. S. authorities to send Dyar to Athens to hear the statement jointly with Marc. Elias talked for several days, admitting a number of past misdeeds and blaming an even greater number on associates. He denied that he had made much money out of narcotics (at that very moment he had a cash balance of a quarter of a million dollars with the Athens branch of the American Express Company, and that was only one of several bank accounts). He denied that he had ever sent drugs to the United States. He denied that George had ever been connected with the business. "It is the American police who are making incessant efforts to have me prosecuted and brought to dishonor," he complained, a statement that Dyar found it impossible to deny. Moses was in Athens at the time, too, and after listening to Elias, Dyar and Marc questioned him for a while. He added to the record a good many details that Elias had conveniently forgotten. When Elias learned that the French had no intention of letting George back in, and that Moses had blabbed, he refused to sign his statement; Moses was glad to sign his.

After this dubious success at being candid, Elias resolved that in the future he would deny everything, and that meanwhile he would become so powerful a figure that no one would dare even bring up the subject of narcotics in his presence. His old friend and ex-employer, George's father-in-law, Euripides Mavromatis, had certain good-looking mining concessions up in Macedonia. With the money that not only Elias, but also Nasso and George, were able to invest, developing the mines was no problem at all. In 1938 (the year Elias wrote the Hamburg authorities that he was unable to afford a trip to Germany), the United States commercial attaché in Athens reported to the Secretary of Commerce that "the most significant new development in Greek mines is the rapid rise of the Eliopoulos group, with a million and a half dollar investment." He went on to detail the holdings of the group, which included several bauxite mines, the marble quarry from which the marble for the Parthenon had been taken, several properties that showed considerable evidence of being rich in gold, other mines producing chromite, pyrolusite, and barites, and a chemical works devoted to converting the products of these latter mines into commercially salable material. The commercial attaché did not add, probably because it was none of his business, that Elias was on intimate terms with a number of cabinet members, and was a center of the social life in the Athens haute monde. George and Nasso, of course, shared this good fortune. Elias liked to keep his money in the family.

Bauxite, which is an aluminum ore, was the Eliopouloses' most profitable line of business; their principal customers were the German and the British governments. And so, when war was declared by England on Germany in 1939, Elias did not allow himself to become provoked. For a man who owns a bauxite mine in a neutral country, there never has been a bad war or a good peace. In 1940, however, the Italians attacked Greece, and Elias's sense of well being began to deteriorate. Still, the Greek army did well enough against the Italians to permit him to feel patriotic. In the early days of the war he was sent by his government to Moscow, on a diplomatic passport, to purchase 100,000 tons of wheat for the army, a mission he completed successfully. He only became seriously disturbed in 1941, when the Germans decided to help the Italians out. Then, with characteristic thoroughness, he made new plans. He and George, he decided, were to flee to America, where they would impersonate homeless refugees who were anxious to help the Allies in any way possible. To give this story substance, Elias ordered a steamship he owned, the *Konstantinos H*, to sail immediately for the United States. Nasso, the hard-boiled brother, was to remain in Athens and make friends with the Nazis, who were obviously going to take over the family mines. Then, just two or three days before the Germans arrived in Athens, George and his wife and daughter, and Elias and his wife—part of Elias's rehabilitation had been ditching his mistress and marrying a Greek girl—sailed for Alexandria. Their departure was not so hasty that Elias had neglected to include in his luggage nine thousand dollars worth of gold bullion, a number of representative specimens from his large collection of stocks and bonds, and a plentiful supply of cash.

11 *An American visit*

Elias had to do a little fast talking before he got to the
United States. No sooner had he and George stepped
ashore at Alexandria in the middle of May 1941, than
representatives of Russell Pasha, who was still very much
on the *qui vive,* greeted them politely and carried them
off to the nearest police station. Elias was well prepared
for this emergency. One of his traveling companions from
Greece had been the brother-in-law of the Greek ambassador to Cairo. He also was able to point out, quite truth-
fully, that before Greece had been invaded he had sold a
good deal of bauxite to the British government; he neglected to add that he had sold just as much to the Germans. Between the diplomatic influence that was exerted
in his behalf, and his record of activity on behalf of the
Allies, Russell Pasha became convinced that he was no
longer a menace to society. He and George were promptly
released; the problem then was to get visas to the United
States. Under normal circumstances getting American
visas would have been a good deal more difficult than ap-
peasing Russell Pasha; in fact it would have been impossible. Both Elias and George appeared on an interna-

tional blacklist issued by the Narcotics Bureau, and consuls were strictly enjoined from letting any member of this select group enter the United States. Elias had this problem under control, too. On Greek passports the names of the bearers are written in both Greek and Latin characters. The eta, which is the first letter of Eliopoulos, looks very much like a Latin H. In Latin characters, the name was spelled Iliopoulos on the passport. To doubly confound this confusion, Elias persuaded a harried clerk in the Alexandria consulate that the Latin spelling was a mistake, and that the name really was Heliopoulos. Caught between this double talk, and the pressure brought by a Greek diplomat in Washington, another old buddy of Elias, the consul at Alexandria never got around to checking the blacklist closely enough to find out who Elias and George were. In June they sailed aboard a British ship for a small port in South Africa. From there they took another ship to Capetown. From there they took still another ship to Trinidad. From Trinidad Elias and his wife flew to Miami, and then took the train to New York, arriving August 4. George, and his family, in more leisurely fashion, waited for the S.S. *Uruguay,* and arrived in New York August 11. Elias moved into the Hotel Stanhope, and on August 15, signed a two year lease for rooms 1006 and 1008 at $175 a month. At his request the management put a clause in the lease giving him the right to cancel it at ninety days' notice in the event the war in Europe ended. George already had reservations at the Hotel Buckingham when he got in; so highly had he been recommended to the hotel that the president of the corporation which owned it met him at the dock when he arrived. Both brothers signed their registration cards Iliopoulos.

It took a couple of months for Harry J. Anslinger, the United States Commissioner of Narcotics, to learn that George and Elias were in the country. Anslinger is a bull-necked Pennsylvania Dutchman with black eyes and an implacable aversion for letting any narcotics trafficker, past, present or future, go his way in peace. He was just as angry at the Eliopoulos brothers in 1941 as he had been in 1931, and since the Narcotics Bureau of the Treasury Department, which he had headed ever since it was organized in 1930, is considered in informed circles to be as deadly a police force as any in the world, he had ample resources for making his choler felt. The very day he learned of the brothers' presence, narcotics agents in New York interviewed the managers of the Stanhope and the Buckingham, and were able to report back that George and Elias were considered—rightly enough—to be "very well-educated, polished and important men of the world." From this time on the brothers were carefully watched. Their bank accounts and financial holdings were subjected to minute investigation; the Post Office was requested to report the return addresses on all mail coming their way, and the addressees of all mail they sent out; the hotels were persuaded to furnish lists of all phone numbers they called through the hotel switchboards; the records of the bureau for 1930, 1931 and 1932 were combed for material that might be useful in getting an indictment; Dyar, who happened to be in the country, was put to racking his memory, and all traffickers or ex-traffickers who were known to have had, or were suspected of having had, dealings with the brothers were questioned extensively. It was not until October 28 that Elias and George were picked up for questioning; Elias had been in Mobile for a week previously, looking over the *Kon-*

stantinos H, which had put in there for an overhaul, prior to being chartered to the Maritime Commission. Neither brother gave his questioners much satisfaction. Both attributed their arrival in the United States under the name of Heliopoulos to an easily understandable clerical error. Elias stoutly maintained that he had led a decorous life ever since 1932, and that even in his indecorous days, he had had no dealings with the United States. George insisted that he never had been in the narcotics business at all. Both agreed to be photographed, but declined to be fingerprinted. It was obvious to the narcotics agents that any information that could be used against the brothers would not come from them.

Confessions by the Eliopoulos brothers, however, were not essential. Among the well-known traffickers who were asked for information about George and Elias was Louis (Fish) Adelman, who was serving a ten-year sentence for dope peddling that had been imposed in 1939. Fish was feeling rather mellow at this point; he had just finished testifying for the prosecution in another important narcotics case, and as a result of his testimony several notorious characters had gone to prison. He was expecting a commutation of his sentence almost any time. When he was shown photographs of George and Elias he identified them immediately as fellows he had known in Paris in 1930, and who still owed him $19,000 for drugs he had bought but never received. In lucid detail he recalled a shipment of 100 kilograms of heroin that he and Sam Bernstein had purchased, and that had been seized in July, 1930, aboard the S.S. *Innoku* in Hoboken. A rapid check of the bureau's files revealed the circumstance of the *Innoku* seizure, and further showed that Bernstein had been indicted for this very shipment, but had never come

to trial for it, because the government had been unable
to secure sufficient evidence. Adelman's wife, Ida, who
had been with her husband on a second business trip to
Paris, also remembered meeting both Eliopouloses. Bernstein was serving time just then, but he was expecting no
commutation of his sentence, so he wasn't feeling mellow.
He refused to commit himself. The Adelman testimony
seemed sufficiently conclusive though, and the government took the case before the Federal Grand Jury in
Trenton. On November 18, Elias, George, and the absent
Nasso were indicted for conspiring to introduce narcotics
illegally into the United States; Adelman, the day previously, had received a presidential pardon. On November
21 the brothers were picked up at their respective hotels; they were taken to New Jersey, booked, and held in
$25,000 bail each. They didn't manage to raise the bail
until December 2; meanwhile they stayed behind bars.
In the middle of December the Justice Department ended
their stay in the United States; the brothers surrendered
to the Immigration authorities at Ellis Island, and were
released, pending deportation proceedings, in one thousand dollars bail each. The Immigration people, however,
agreed to hold up action until the Narcotics Bureau had
had its innings.

An extremely nice legal point was involved in attempting to imprison Elias and George in 1942 for an offense
presumably committed in 1930. Ordinarily there would
have been no question of a trial; the ten-year statute of
limitations would have run out, as the defense, indeed,
claimed it had. The government's position was based on a
section in the law which suspends operation of the statute
of limitations during the time the defendants are absent
from the jurisdiction of the United States, which in this

case had been the entire period since the commission of the crime. The defense countered this argument by claiming that "absence" as defined by the law implied prior presence, and that the brothers had never been present. In March these tricky arguments were heard by Judge Philip Forman, and all other legal activity was suspended while he pondered the matter. He finally gave his decision in July. It was in favor of the defense, and he threw the indictments out. A less relentless man than Anslinger would have given up at this point, but Anslinger had been advised by his legal staff that in the Southern District of New York, as opposed to the District of New Jersey, there was a body of precedent favorable to the prosecution, and that an indictment in that district might stand up. And so the bureau now devoted its efforts to digging up an attempt by the brothers to smuggle narcotics in the Southern District of New York. Meanwhile, Anslinger noted, the bureau's activities were causing George and Elias considerable annoyance, and since annoyance was exactly what Anslinger wanted to cause them, he was not too displeased with the result of his work so far.

For a while the search for a suitable case in the Southern District of New York got nowhere. Big Nose Willie Fleischman, in retirement in Miami, was interviewed at length, but he would not commit himself any further than to say that once, in Paris, Elias gave him a pound of smoking opium as a personal gift. Little Augie, back in the money as a bookmaker, numbers king and general big wheel on the Lower East Side, also was courteous but uncommunicative. Sam Bernstein was still being worked on, but so far had contributed little of value, and Jake Polakiewitz, who was quite willing to talk, didn't know enough to do any good. Then in September, in the course of routine operations, the Chicago district office of the bureau learned that Albert Schwartz was being held in the Milwaukee jail on charges of operating a confidence game. Schwartz was a familiar face to the bureau. Although he had fled to Europe in June, 1931, when his trunk, with 25 kilos of heroin in it, had been seized on Pier 95, North River, fresh off the *Conte Biancamano,* he had finally come back to the United States, had been arrested for the *Conte Biancamano* job, and had been sentenced to seven and a half years. He had emerged from prison only a couple of years before, and had been operating his confidence game with such persistence ever since, that by this time he was wanted in Denver, San Francisco, Oklahoma City, St. Paul, San Diego, Lancaster, Pa., Utica, Santa Barbara and Chicago. If not the most accomplished con man in the world, Schwartz was obviously one of the most experienced fugitives.

Still as a matter of routine, the Chicago office sent a man to Milwaukee to talk to Schwartz, and since one of the routine questions every trafficker was asked at this point was about the Eliopoulos brothers, the Chicago agent asked it. To his surprise and gratification, Schwartz replied without hesitation that he knew the brothers well, had worked for them for years, and that the heroin seized on Pier 95 was stuff they had sold him. Pier 95 is right in the heart of the Southern District of New York; a New York agent lost no time in getting to Milwaukee to hear Schwartz's story. Once he had heard it he persuaded the Milwaukee authorities to let him carry Schwartz back to New York. In New York Schwartz was confronted by the Adelmans, who remembered seeing him in Paris. The *Conte Biancamano* case seemed even better than the *Innoku* case; the United States Attorney had no trouble at all, early in November, getting indictments against George and Elias. On November 5 they were arrested again. George, the arresting agent noted in his report, "cried, begged and shouted" when he was picked up. Elias remained unruffled, but referred to the District Supervisor of Narcotics as "chief of the Gestapo." They were arraigned the following day, and George was held in $3000 bail, Elias in $5000. They produced the money immediately. What with the state of the calendar in the Southern District, it wasn't until February 1, 1943, that the arguments about the statute of limitations were heard by Judge Vincent L. Leibell. He didn't have to think as long as Judge Forman. He returned a decision favorable to the government two weeks later. Because of the calendar, however, the trial itself had to be put off several times, and meanwhile Sam Bernstein had decided to talk, and had told all about the 500-kilogram *Alesia* seizure in Brooklyn in December, 1930. The bureau decided to get an indictment in the Eastern District of New York too. The indictment was returned on May 5, and the brothers were arrested for the third time on that date. They were arraigned May 7, and each produced the requisite $5000 bail. Hearings on the statute of limitations were held May 17, and Judge Matthew T. Abruzzo set something of a speed record by returning a decision favorable to the government the following day. On May 26 the trial began.

The trial lasted eleven days. The principal witnesses for the government were Bernstein, Adelman and Schwartz, all of whom described in much detail their association with the brothers. Under cross examination none of these stories was seriously disturbed. For the defense the only witnesses were George and Elias themselves. They made a poor showing on the stand, and were tripped up constantly in the cross examination. The jury absented itself for only a few hours; at 11:10 P.M. on June 11 it declared both defendants guilty. The defense attorneys then renewed their point about the statute of limitations, and Judge Abruzzo agreed to study the matter again. This time he did not hurry. It wasn't until October that he finally rendered his decision, favorable to the defense. "My view is," he said, "that on everything else in this case, the defendants are not entitled to anything in their favor. I believe that the question of fact has been passed upon and the jury had sufficient evidence to find them guilty of the crime charged. I do not see any reason for disturbing it [the verdict] on that ground, or any reason for disturbing it on the ground that it [the trial] should have been adjourned until after the war." But, he said, absence as defined by the statute did indeed presuppose prior presence, and therefore the verdict had to be set aside. This just about ended any hope Anslinger had of sending the brothers to prison. The Southern District case had been put off the calendar until the Eastern District case was disposed of; there seemed little likelihood now that it would go back on. There was considerable talk of making an appeal, but nothing ever came of it. Arguments weren't presented to the Circuit Court of Appeals until October, 1945, and then the appeal was thrown out because the papers had not been filed within 30 days after Judge Abruzzo's decision. Finally, in October, 1947, the Southern District indictments were also thrown out, and a month later the solicitor general formally advised Anslinger that he would not appeal this

decision. Anslinger tried to dig up a case that would warrant an indictment in Canada, where the limitations laws
are different, but he was unable to manage it.

For a few months after the trial, George and Elias went,
more or less, into hiding. Elias moved from the Hotel
Stanhope to the Hotel Salisbury where, presumably, he
was unknown. His wife was no longer with him. Early in
1943, when the Southern District case was looking pretty
sinister, she had developed an acute headache, and had
gone to California to cure it. She hasn't been heard from
since. George and his family retired to a small town in
New Jersey, and a narcotics agent who went to see him in
April, 1944, reported that he was in poor health; he was
unshaven, and was wearing a dirty shirt, a torn sweater
and frayed trousers. He pulled himself * together
soon enough, however. By March, 1945, he had taken a
shave, sent his clothes to the cleaner, and moved into the
Adlon Apartments at 200 West 54th Street. Elias, a less
sensitive type, had recovered long before this. By March,
1945, he had succeeded so well in recapturing his self-
confidence that he had just about persuaded the United
States Bureau of Mines to send him to Greece to supervise the rehabilitation of his properties there. His mines
had been blown up, he said, by the Germans, because of
his splendid record of cooperation with the Allies. Anslinger put the kibosh on this scheme quickly enough,
and two months later he was gratified to see a report from
Army Intelligence in Greece, informing the U. S. Government that the Eliopoulos mines had been blown up by
Greek guerillas because of their services to the Nazis, and
containing a brief account of the gay and profitable life
Nasso had led in Athens during the German occupation.
When all legal proceedings against him were finally

dropped, in November, 1947, Elias was very happy to sail back home to rejoin Nasso. In December, 1947, the Immigration Bureau renewed its deportation action against George, who had declared his intention of remaining here. He had established an office in the Wall Street district, and was acting as his brothers' American representative. At the first hearing he was ordered out, but he appealed the case, and it wasn't until four years ago that he was finally forced to leave the country.

From time to time the Narcotics Bureau attempts, with mixed success, to bring its dossiers on Elias's co-conspirators up to date, and on the basis of information received Anslinger has no reason to believe that many of them have suffered much for their activities. Sam Bernstein, of course, did go to prison, and in June, 1944, he died of cancer in the Bellevue prison ward. Louis Adelman and Albert Schwartz both served time, also; they are now free men and reformed characters. Leonoff-Goldstein was hounded all over Europe during the thirties, and finally dropped out of sight. The rest, though, seemed to have done rather well. Augie was still rich, powerful and unrepentant when he died in April, 1949, of cancer of the throat, shortly after returning from his winter vacation at Hot Springs, Virginia. J—— is a member of the Légion d'Honneur. L——, when last heard from, was a respected businessman in France. Paul Mechelaere has been unreported for years, but when last heard from he was in Antwerp and still in the traffic. John Voyatzis was never molested in his mountain village, where he enjoyed a patriarchal existence. Elie Abouissac retired quietly to Florence in the early thirties, where the fortune he had acquired made him a distinguished citizen. David Gourievidis spent a number of years in China, fabulously rich and still in the same old business; then, when the Communists approached his headquarters he withdrew to South America, where he had been thoughtfully stowing his assets for some time. Kosta Belokas, so shadowy a figure that no policeman ever even had a photograph of him, has disappeared completely. Seja Moses never went to prison. George and Nasso Eliopoulos are in Greece today. Both are wealthy men with a variety of profitable business connections, especially bauxite, chromium and nickel mines in northern Greece and on Melos, an island in the Aegean. Elias died early in 1955 in Athens. Up to his death he was doing as well, or better, than his two brothers. One recent project, that Anslinger scotched in the nick of time, was a projected ECA loan to help finance their bauxite venture. And as for the thousands of men and women all over the world who first became drug addicts because of the work of the Eliopoulos brothers, many of them are still around too, but it is safe to say that few of them are prosperous, or healthy, or happy.

PART THREE

The Counterfeiters

¹ Mr. Livingston takes a trip

For anyone with a gourmand's indiscriminate relish for crime, Paris, in the four or five years immediately following the Liberation, must have been paradise. Parisian unrighteousness during those years would scarcely have suited a connoisseur; qualitatively it was, on the whole, unimaginative, even vulgar. Quantitatively, though, it was magnificent; it came in every shape and size, and in superb profusion. The fortunes and habits, the minds and governments of men had been so violently dislocated by the war that hundreds of thousands of people who, under more auspicious circumstances, might never have done anything more wicked than throw paving stones at the Garde Mobile on May Day, found themselves embroiled in criminal intrigues of the most intricate kind. The vortex of this welter of illegality was the black market. The black market had come into being, of course, because so many sorts of goods were hard to get, and because French currency was "soft"—in other words was not, in the estimation of the public, worth as much as the government said it was. Most black market transactions were either in scarce commodities or foreign exchange. However the mere existence of a widespread clandestine apparatus for trafficking in contraband made operations relatively simple for criminals of a much more ambitious variety than squalid Algerian money changers or avaricious Norman dairy farmers. The black market was an admirable medium through which to pass such worthwhile items as a couple of ounces of heroin, or a handful of smuggled diamonds, or a consignment of machine guns for the Stern Gang, or a roll of counterfeit hundred-dollar bills.

Of the kinds of major crime that waxed and multiplied in Paris between 1945 and 1950, perhaps the most flourishing was counterfeiting. Almost every circumstance combined to make this true. The incentive was greater than it had ever been, because it was profitable to counterfeit a great many things besides the domestic currency, which in normal times is about the only item worth a counterfeiter's attention. Because such basic commodities as food, clothing and gasoline were being rationed, it was lucrative to counterfeit ration stamps; because for a while, American cigarettes fetched such high prices, one group found it expedient to counterfeit Camel packages; because, in many railroad stations it took several hours on queue to buy a ticket, there was even a lively traffic in counterfeit tickets; the increase in smuggling, and in the number of homeless persons, made counterfeit passports and identification papers fetch a premium price; and, last and most important, the unprecedented fact that some currencies were "hard" and some "soft," made counterfeiting foreign money, especially American dollars and Swiss francs, an extremely rewarding enterprise. (For obvious reasons, foreign counterfeit was considerably easier to pass than domestic, and so the workmanship did not have to be nearly so tidy.)

The opportunity to counterfeit was just as inflated as the motive, although ordinarily counterfeiting is one of the more difficult crimes both to perpetrate and to get away with. To manufacture counterfeit requires a fairly costly and elaborate physical plant, and a group of skilled technicians; to distribute counterfeit is usually a tedious business, because it involves fobbing the product off on the public one or two units at a time, and it is a risky business because such an extensive series of petty transactions leaves a plain trail for the police to follow. Neither of these limitations applied with any force in France in the late forties. During the Resistance every other bush in the maquis, so to speak, had concealed a clandestine print shop and a full complement of desperate mechanics, patriotically occupied with forging identification papers, ration tickets and money. Enough of this machinery and personnel was still at loose ends to solve most production problems. Distribution was even less vexing than manufacture. Thanks to the black market, the man who wanted to pass counterfeit no longer had to spend several tiresome weeks traveling about the country, buying a pack of cigarettes here, a magazine there and a pair of socks some other place. All he had to do was take his wad, the thicker the better, into the black market, and dispose of it in one piece like a gentleman.

That, then, was roughly the posture of affairs on June 19, 1947 when M. I. Soederlund, a lean and experienced detective who, for twenty years had been the American Express Company's chief special agent in Europe, received word that a counterfeit hundred-dollar American Express Company traveler's cheque had been put into circulation. The rumor came, as did much of the information, true and false, that the American Express Company and the

French police were to receive on the subject during the next couple of years, from informers, a class of individuals who, like counterfeiters, had thrived under the Occupation, and of whom there was now a definite surplus. On June 20 and 21 and 22 and 23, the rumors continued with increased insistence. On June 24 a report arrived from Brussels that a man had actually showed up on the Bourse with a counterfeit hundred-dollar cheque but had vanished when told it was a phony. On June 25 the police in Nice arrested four Parisian malefactors who were attempting to purchase jewelry with one of the counterfeits. They were found to have seventy-four more of them in their possession. On June 26, a man was arrested in a café on the Champs Elysées during the apéritif hour by a police agent to whom he was attempting to sell ten of the counterfeits. That same day the first of the counterfeits to show up in actual circulation arrived at the Paris office of the American Express. That evening a report was forwarded to American Express headquarters in New York that the general aspect of the counterfeit cheque was good, although the color was a trifle pale; the watermark in the paper was faked—in other words, printed; the planchettes, or heavy, opaque disks, that are built right into the paper in a genuine cheque, were also printed, and the red serial numbers were a little dark. The counterfeit cheques were apparently being sold wholesale on the black market at the rate of seventy-five or eighty francs to the dollar. (Retail, of course, they were drawing the same price as genuine cheques, something around 250 francs per dollar. The official rate of exchange at the time was less than two hundred francs per dollar. The fact that the retailers were operating on so much greater a profit margin than the wholesalers was not surprising, since the wholesalers were handling a large volume at a small risk, while the retailers were in precisely the opposite position.)

During the next three weeks it became painfully clear that the counterfeiters had gotten a good head start. Bogus cheques turned up all over Western Europe, mostly one or two at a time, in the hands of citizens who had acquired them more or less in good faith—"more or less" because, although they had bought the cheques in the belief they were authentic, they had patronized the black market to make the purchases. On July 3 a Lucerne bank refused to cash one of them for an unknown woman, who thereupon beat a retreat, abandoning the cheque in her haste. On the same day twenty of them arrived at the New York Clearing House, and were traced back from there through a garment district check-cashing establishment, a Lower East Side jeweler, and several other intermediaries, to the pilot of an Air France transatlantic plane. The following week they began appearing in Sweden and Holland. On July 15 a man was arrested in Basle with seven of them; it was established that he had acquired them in Strasbourg.

Counterfeiting traveler's cheques is an occupation of which the American Express Company, to put it mildly, disapproves. Traveler's cheques are the backbone of the company's business; from them, over the years, it has drawn a substantial part of its revenue and an even greater share of its reputation. American Express Company traveler's cheques, when properly signed and countersigned, are negotiable on sight almost anywhere in the world; in many places they are regarded as being as good as, if not better than, cash money. The company has no obligation to make good on counterfeits, although it sometimes does if they have been, demonstrably, accepted in the course of routine business—which does not include having been bought on the black market. Therefore counterfeiters are no more able to threaten American Express with financial ruin by forging cheques than they are the government of the United States by forging twenty-dollar bills. The important loss counterfeiters can inflict on the company is to the integrity of its promissory obligations, and so the company maintains a good-sized and costly investigative department whose major function is to demonstrate convincingly to all would-be forgers that messing with traveler's cheques is a perilous folly.

As soon as it became evident, early in July, that the European counterfeiters were very much in earnest, J. K. Livingston, vice president and secretary of the company, a dignified elderly gentleman with a gray mustache and a well-developed aptitude and zest for sleuthing, left for Paris to supervise the hunt for the criminals. He arrived there on July 18 and, while he was settling himself, the case became lusher and lusher. Dozens of the cheques showed up in ones, twos and threes, and there were several large seizures. On July 22 the Banque de France received fifty of the counterfeits which had been confiscated by customs officers a couple of days previously at Vallorbe, on the Swiss border. The confiscation had taken place because, contrary to currency regulations, the cheques had not been declared; the customs men had had no idea that they were counterfeit, so they had let the man who was carrying them go on through into Switzerland. On July 29, in Geneva, three men were arrested with thirty of the counterfeits while attempting to buy jewelry with them. On August 5 a Geneva bank found it had one hundred of the counterfeits, bearing ninety-six different signatures, which had been personally deposited by the first secretary of a South American legation in Paris, who had carried them across the border in his inviolable diplomatic luggage. He had, of course, obtained them on the black market in Paris, but the attempt to trace their original source petered out in a medley of denials, cross-charges and buck-passing by the miscellaneous money changers and middle men involved. That same week individual cheques, all carrying a signature that looked like "Rinc," began appearing in a series of cities and towns in northern Italy, and continued to do so for a month or six weeks.

From where Livingston sat, at this point, the case couldn't have been more bewildering. In eight or ten countries almost a hundred people, of heaven knows how many different nationalities, professions and stations of life, falling into thirty or forty separate groups, had been tied up with the counterfeits, and, in many cases, questioned or even arrested. Yet, except that they were all handling the same issue of bad cheques, there was so far not the smallest visible connection between any of the groups. Unfortunately for the counterfeiters, this was precisely the sort of challenge that filled Livingston with zeal. He was able to discern through the murk that the obvious source of the counterfeits was Paris, and that, therefore, most if not all of the parties fingered so far were very likely mere peddlers, not the manufacturers and jobbers he was anxious to catch. In Paris itself the case was already in exceptionally capable hands. It had been turned over to the two most able, if overworked, counterfeiting experts in France, Commissaire Principal Louis Poirier, of the Paris police, an enormous, mustachioed operative, and Commissaire Principal Emile Benhamou of the Sureté Nationale, a wiry little Algerian. Soederlund, a proficient investigator who enjoyed their confidence, was assisting in the researches. One of the most enterprising of the Parisian *juges d' instruction,* or examining magistrates, Marcel Frapier, a gentleman who, like Livingston, was captivated by the very intricacy of the affair, had been assigned to it. American Express itself had become a *partie civile,* in which capacity it was permitted to be present, in the person of its lawyer, at the questioning of suspects and witnesses, and to suggest lines of inquiry to the police and Judge Frapier.

Under these circumstances, Livingston could be confident that both leg work and interrogations were being capably handled. He decided that the interests of justice and his company would best be served by directing most of his attention, and that of whatever other American Express personnel was available, to the complex and essential office work connected with the case: Securing through the International Criminal Police Commission the cooperation of the police counterfeiting squads in all the countries of Western Europe, so that whatever information turned up anywhere could reach Paris rapidly; comparing the signatures on all the counterfeits that appeared with each other, and with the handwriting of the suspects; compiling an elaborate, cross-indexed list of all the people whose names, at any time, were mentioned in connection with the case, in an effort to establish some relationship among them. Poirier, Benhamou and Frapier were delighted to have these burdens removed from their overloaded backs. During September and October there was plenty of office work to do. The cheques kept coming in from all over Europe, and each time one did a whole new set of names had to be scrutinized and entered in the Who's Who, often with the result of making things less intelligible than ever.

However, beginning at the end of October and continuing for more than two years, during all of which Livingston remained on the scene, devoting his full time to the case, the main outlines of the plot slowly did take shape. An accurate account of the investigation, although fascinating, could not be given without mapping the countless blind alleys up which the detectives were led; without furnishing scores of biographical sketches of such beguiling, but wholly peripheral, characters as a nervous Rumanian night club musician, a larcenous ex-GI from Schenectady and an overdressed Hungarian ballerina traveling under six separate aliases; without detailing numbers of other counterfeiting plots, in dollars, in Deutschmarks, in pesetas, in bread ration stamps, in notes on the Banque de L'Afrique Occidentale; without touching on smuggling in the Basque country; the suicide of a bankrupt Corsican gangster, and the political activities of various dissident Yugoslavs. As in most successful police work, information was picked up crumb by crumb, and never once was the investigation enlivened by a rapier-like flash of reasoning that immediately dissolved all difficulties. Nevertheless the results were most gratifying, particularly from the point of view of sheer bulk. When the affair finally got to court, in March, 1950, fifty-nine defendants, of thirteen different nationalities, were under indictment, fifty of whom were convicted and sentenced to jail terms ranging from nine years down, and to fines as high, in a number of instances, as six million francs. As *partie civile* American Express was awarded damages (uncollectable) of twenty million francs. Not the least remarkable feature of the trial was the impossibility of finding any courtroom in Paris with adequate facilities for accommodating that many defendants, plus their thirty-five lawyers, plus the crowds of newspapermen who attended. The trial was, from all reports, a scene whose congestion was unparalleled in the history of French jurisprudence. Stripped of its excessive ornamentation, however, the conspiracy itself was relatively simple to understand.

2 Jake and his pals

It all started shortly after New Year's, 1947. Loitering in Paris at that time was a brisk young New Yorker of the form-fitting-navy-blue-topcoat, broad-brimmed-gray-fedora, iridescent-necktie set, named Jake. Jake's ostensible line of work was "furs," a term that, in common with "precious stones," "import-export" and other callings favored by gentlemen of his species, was comprehensive enough to include peddling nylon stockings and ball-point pens on the black market, smuggling diamonds out of Amsterdam, and shipping hand grenades to Palestine in cases labeled "farm machinery." Jake was not ordinarily a loiterer, but at this moment, although his imagination was teeming with projects, he was unable to afford any of them. He had just been taken for one million francs in a floating blackjack game.

Among the connections Jake had established in the course of his dealings in "furs," was one with a voluble, middle-aged Latvian named Rachmiel—or Michel, as the French insisted on calling him—Hirscovics. Except for a humiliating interlude in the middle twenties, when he had been obliged to work as head waiter at Ciro's, Hirscovics had devoted his life to free-lance fulminations in behalf of whatever political party or government could pay for his services. He considered himself a master of intrigue, and in order to induce the world to share this belief, he faithfully waxed his mustache and wore, even in July, a majestic, if somewhat frayed, greatcoat with an astrakhan collar, although at the time Jake got to know him he more frequently affected the uniform of a captain in the Red Army, and claimed to be military attaché to the Soviet Embassy. (This was plainly a preposterous assertion, although he probably had run some errands for the Reds.) Hirscovics, too, was insolvent in January, 1947. His latest transaction, a piece of private enterprise, had been no more rewarding than Jake's attempt at blackjack. He had, with a good deal of skill, managed to sell a large number of nonexistent tractors to a gullible Frenchman who had found it impossible to buy existing ones through orthodox channels. The Frenchman had paid off in ten-thousand-franc notes. Hirscovics was congratulating himself on his shrewd handling of this affair when the French government, as an anti-hoarding measure, called in all ten-thousand-franc notes. Hirscovics gamely attempted to convert his, having had years of experience at making specious explanations. He had been able to talk fast enough to avoid incarceration, but not to keep his profits.

What had brought Jake and Hirscovics together was a profound sympathy that they shared for the extremist groups in Palestine. Of the sincerity of their ultra-Zionism there can be little doubt; such sentiments, involving, as they did, arms-running and passport forgery, were potentially most lucrative. (Anti-Franco enthusiasm was also rife in the European underworld. The habit of equating crime with political idealism, which had grown up under the Nazis, was too convenient to break.) In casting about for an economically sound method of helping to liberate Palestine, Hirscovics and Jake hit upon the notion of counterfeiting traveler's cheques which could then be used to purchase arms for the extremists there. Jake was quite certain that he could promote, from "import-export" acquaintances not addicted to blackjack, sufficient cash to finance a double play that could be as spectacularly profitable as that. In the course of extensive European travels, he had acquired much precise information about where such arms could be obtained and how they could be shipped. He started at once to secure the necessary backing, and at the same time he performed the routine, but essential, job of acquiring a genuine, unsigned cheque to serve as the model for the counterfeit. One day, at the height of the rush hour, he sauntered cheerfully into American Express headquarters on the Rue Scribe, purchased a book of eight hundred-dollar cheques, and then, by the judicious use of legerdemain as he signed the cheques in the presence of the teller, avoided signing the last one in the book.

While Jake was thus organizing the front office, Hirscovics set about recruiting a technical squad to execute the counterfeiting itself. He engaged the services of another militant Jew, Jacques Frydman, a dashing redheaded lad who was fresh out of La Santé prison, where he had been confined for committing burglary while absent without leave from the French army. Frydman got in touch with an old jailmate, a stout and florid linotypist named René Chauvet. Chauvet communicated with his bosom friend, Roger David, a dour stick-up man. David unearthed, finally, the man they were looking for, Paul Considére, who was the business representative for a group of printers firmly established in the counterfeiting business. The four middlemen, Hirscovics, Frydman, Chauvet and David, who were needed to put Jake, representing the bankroll, in touch with Considére, representing the mechanics, were by no means an excessive number for such an enterprise. A major difficulty encountered by the detectives who attempted to unravel this affair was precisely the one that makes almost any business deal, illegal or not, hard to follow; the people who actually did something were always outnumbered by, and far less conspicuous than, the people who performed introductions, arranged appointments, made telephone calls and, in general, bustled about with soiled scraps of paper in their pockets and knowledgeable looks on their faces.

The first conference with Considére occurred, around the middle of March, in Hirscovics's rooms at the Pension George V, 26 Rue Washington. This outwardly modest and respectable boardinghouse catered to a select clientele that consisted exclusively of characters anxious to elude the attention of the police; Frydman also was in residence there for a time, and the landlady, apparently, was an old business acquaintance of Considére's from the days when he had been booking agent for a remunerative string of party girls.

Hirscovics had outdone himself in arranging his quarters for the meeting. Into the center of his sitting room, whose decor largely consisted of wallpaper depicting ultramarine cabbage roses adrift in a pale pink mist, he had drawn a circular table, and placed around it a group of chairs whose sole common denominator was upholstery of a particularly abrasive grade of plush. On the table he had arranged several packs of black-market American cigarettes, a row of chipped tumblers, a bottle of vodka for his use, a bottle of blended rye for Jake's and a bottle of cognac for the conferees with less exotic tastes. Considére turned out to be a squat, muscular, yellow-haired individual in his forties, grim of feature, curt and contemptuous of speech and, from the tips of his pointed shoes to the checkered cap on his head, strictly the old pro. When Hirscovics, assuming the chair, proposed a moving toast to British confusion in the Middle East, he sneered. When Hirscovics then went on to deliver some extended introductory remarks about being firmly united, through enlightened self-interest, in a glorious common cause, he yawned, and finally interrupted to declare that political oratory fatigued him. This uncouth behavior, although shocking to the sensibilities of the others, did have the effect of inducing them to talk business. Jake produced his virgin cheque, and Considére, after examining it, said that he had access to technicians who could make an excellent photo-engraving from it; a press on which it could be run off, and an ample supply of paper. The only problem, as he saw it, was whether Jake had enough money to pay for this costly industrial process.

That, in fact, was precisely the problem, and to its solution the several parties devoted not only most of that afternoon, but a sizable number of other afternoons, over a period of some weeks. There was not only the size of Jake's payment to Considére to be haggled over, but also the crucial detail of what installments were to be paid when. The precise amounts that were finally agreed to were never accurately determined by either the police or American Express. Indications were that the total sum pledged by Jake was in the neighborhood of three-quarters of a million francs (about four thousand dollars), one-third of which was to be paid immediately as an inducement to the photographer-engraver; one-third to be paid, for the purchase of paper, when the completed plates had been physically introduced into evidence; and one-third to be paid upon delivery of the finished product. In the course of these negotiations Hirscovics and Chauvet, mostly at Considére's initiative, were gradually pushed into the background, Hirscovics because he was, in Considére's characteristically brutal phrase, "an ancient and incredible windbag," and Chauvet because of an infirm intellect and an immoderate fondness for brandy, under whose influence he tended to babble confidingly to anyone at all.

Jake had little difficulty in raising the amount of the first installment from the acquaintances he had already sounded out, and Considére carried the unsigned cheque to one Pierre Benor, a mild man who worked on army maps as a photo-engraver for the National Geographical Institute. Benor, having a private darkroom at the institute, could do anything he pleased there; when he turned on the red light in the corridor over the darkroom door no one would dare bother him for hours on end. It was a good thing he had such a secure workshop, since making plates for the cheque was an intricate operation. Four of them were required, one for the blue on the face of the cheque, one for the purple on the face, one for the black, and one for the light blue background for the serial numbers. In addition he had to do a vast amount of retouching to delete the serial numbers, and the planchettes and the watermark in the paper. It was a job that took several weeks.

Presently Considére showed up with the plates, and demanded the second installment. While Benor had been toiling in his darkroom, Jake had been airing himself down Grenoble way, with the object of locating someone to meet this demand. He had come up with a manufacturer of ladies' handbags from that metropolis, Julien Wegrow. Wegrow, until American relatives of his put him in touch with Jake, had been addicted to Palestine, but not in any large way to larceny. His business, a moderately prosperous one, was quite legitimate. It would be difficult to maintain that his interest in the plot was entirely selfless, but political conviction undoubtedly animated him to a greater extent than it did any other central conspirator. He was a bizarre little man, under five feet high and almost perfectly bald. Both his manners and his taste in dress would have to be described as courtly, and they were objects of helpless admiration to numbers of susceptible ladies in both Grenoble and Paris. To meet the second installment, he produced 160,000 francs in cash and a diamond representing another 100,-000 francs. The diamond was a fake.

That fake diamond put the relationship between Jake and Considére, for the first time, on a realistic basis. However sophisticated Jake may have been in the ballpoint pen traffic, he entered the exalted sphere of big-time professional counterfeiting as a lamb asking to be slaughtered. He had apparently imagined that Considére was simply a sort of printer's agent who would accept a work order, deliver the goods, and then quietly efface himself, leaving Jake to enjoy the profits. This naïve notion Considére was happy to foster. In the original negotiations he had cheerfully guaranteed that Jake and his friends would have exclusive distribution rights to the counterfeits for three months after they came off the press. Obviously he never had the faintest intention of honoring a pledge like that. His associates were not only printers, but experienced and well-connected black marketers. What he had in mind, no doubt, was to extract from Jake all the cash possible, and in return give him only enough of the counterfeits to prevent him from telling tales to the gendarmerie. If Jake was green, however, he was not ineducable. With the advice of Frydman, who was a sharp, observant youth, he began to get the drift along about the time of his Grenoble trip. By then his investment was already large. He wanted to cut his losses. Sticking Considére with the fake diamond was a gesture that not only saved him a hundred thousand francs, but impressed on Considére that he was under suspicion and that any future hanky-panky would be vigorously deplored.

3 *Marcel le Marseillais*

Considére, although he had carefully kept Jake in the dark about it, was by no means the leading light in the printer's group; he was a hired hand whose principal function was to keep his boss anonymous. The boss was Marcel Vignon, a forty-year-old ex-printer who operated a café called Chez Marcel on the Rue Clauzel. (For some obscure reason Vignon, who was born in Toulon, was known in counterfeiting circles as "Marcel le Marseillais." Perhaps the person who so dubbed him had just read an article on the colorful argot of the underworld.) Of all the characters immediately involved with the counterfeit cheques, Vignon was the only one who even came close to being a bona-fide, twenty-four-carat, Senate-Investigating-Committee-type mastermind. He was a tall, swarthy man, with a calm disposition, a candid manner, and a methodical, intelligent way of doing business. A friend of his owned a Webendorfer offset press (manufactured in Mt. Vernon, N.Y.) that had been brought into France for legitimate purposes in 1946, had somehow been diverted, and was now available, at a fixed fee and no questions asked, to anyone who cared to rent it. Vignon had already had occasion to hire it in connection with a profitable little deal in Spanish pesetas—"in behalf of the Loyalist underground," naturally—and he also had some promising transactions pending in reference to Belgian francs and American dollars. (He managed to pull them off successfully before the police caught up with him.) In addition he had handled a great many other issues of counterfeit as a jobber, being a powerful figure in a section of the black market that abounded in Corsicans, the race that traditionally supplies the French underworld with its most savage personnel.

Considére was Vignon's regular front man, and in his permanent stable of technicians were Benor, and a printer named Henri Guitard who was the brightest star in the galaxy, and Vignon's particular friend. Guitard was a small nondescript Parisian, who limped as the result of a war wound for which he was receiving a sixty-five percent disability pension from the government. He was regarded as a hero of the Resistance, having spent most of his time during the Occupation counterfeiting anything and everything that could distress the Nazis. Because of this, and his undoubted technical genius, he was so revered by all his acquaintances that he seldom had to buy himself a drink. One of Guitard's distinguished contributions to the art of counterfeiting had been inventing a process for printing a fake watermark. He used it on the traveler's cheques.

The proprietor of the Webendorfer kept his treasure in a warehouse, and rented it f.o.b. It was incumbent on the lessees to find suitable quarters for it, and carry it there. During May Vignon struck up an acquaintance with an occasional patron of his café who operated a small combination grocery store, coffee shop and bar, with a big cellar underneath it, in Champigny, in the outskirts of Paris. This individual agreed to rent Vignon the cellar for three weeks for twenty thousand francs. Shortly before the first of June, a truck carrying the Webendorfer, under canvas, and Vignon, Guitard and Considére, pulled up to the grocery store. With considerable emphasis Vignon ordered the landlord to make himself scarce for a while, which the latter did with alacrity. The three others thereupon unloaded the press, and sundry rolls of paper and containers of ink, and carried them below ground. Over the course of the next three weeks Vignon and Guitard appeared periodically in Champigny. Their performance there was invariable. They would silently descend into the cellar, and lock the door behind them. Presently the clanking of the press would be heard, and continue uninterrupted for hours. Every so often one or the other of them would knock on the ceiling and demand that sandwiches and coffee or wine be sent down. These were delivered, and paid for, through the narrowest possible opening of the cellar door. They frequently remained below for as long as seventy-two hours on end, sleeping a few hours on bundles of straw, but most of the time running the press. At the end of each session they would leave, first carefully locking the door, as silently as they had come. Late in the evening of June 19, after an especially prolonged session, Considére arrived with the truck. He gave the landlord his twenty thousand francs, and sent him away again. The press was lugged upstairs, heaved aboard, swathed once more in canvas, and returned quietly to its owner. It had produced six thousand counterfeit hundred-dollar cheques during its three subterranean weeks in Champigny.

The plot was now, as Vignon was acutely aware, in its

most critical phase. Now that the counterfeits were actually in existence, the authorities were almost certain to hear about them, through informers, even before the first sample showed up, and that sample would show up, he knew, not more than a week after the first cheque was put on the market. He also knew what would happen then: American Express would send out a warning, accurately describing the counterfeit, to all its branches and to every bank in Europe; in less than a week from that time bank tellers who had previously honored traveler's cheques without a second glance would be giving the beady eye to every one that came into their hands; a few days after that hotel cashiers, airport ticket clerks, jewelry store managers and other habitual handlers of large sums would be in a morbidly suspicious state of mind; in the face of these perils, black market operators would no longer care to have any truck with the cheques, and distribution would degenerate into a laborious, one-at-a-time operation. He had, in short, two weeks at the outside in which to unload his stock, and so the need for haste was extreme. That was why he had never had the smallest intention of honoring the three-month pledge that Jake had exacted. He was worried, though, that Jake would derange his delicate time schedule by running to the authorities, a course of action that Jake, who was becoming increasingly skittish, had threatened to take on a number of occasions. Consequently he had, through Considére, set June 20 as a firm date for delivering a consignment of cheques to Jake, and had even permitted Considére to show Jake a sample cheque before the press run was finished. On June 19, Jake induced Hirscovics, who by then had come to be regarded as eminently expendable, to cash the sample as a test of negotiability. Hirscovics managed without difficulty, which somewhat soothed Jake's jangled nerves.

The June 20 delivery took place in the workroom of a dim millinery shop operated by one of Wegrow's female admirers. Considére, accompanied by David, who was tottering under the weight of a bulky valise, appeared in this musty and cluttered chamber toward the middle of the morning. Frydman and Wegrow were awaiting them. Jake himself felt he had better stay away from this session in case anyone lost his temper. Very little time was spent in the exchange of politenesses. David heaved the suitcase onto a table, squashing a couple of priceless toques in the process, and Considére, after lifting the lid of the valise and allowing Frydman and Wegrow a tantalizing glimpse of the two or three thousand counterfeit cheques inside, indicated that he was ready to receive the third and final installment of the payment Jake had promised to make. Frydman, with wordy apologies, said that Jake had been unable to gather any more cash. Considére rudely uttered the French equivalent of no tickee, no washee. Wegrow, with a burst of righteous indignation, said that the contributions he and Jake had already made had been quite handsome enough. Considére endeavored to paint a pathetic picture of the terrible expenses and risks he had undergone to do this job for his friends. Wegrow, who, being a bona fide businessman, had a great deal more experience than Considére at this sort of whining, painted an even more pathetic picture of the expenses and risks *he* had undergone. Considére reverted to the no tickee, no washee theme. Frydman, still feigning regret, intimated that Jake was prepared to communicate with the authorities within the hour in the event no satisfactory arrangement was reached. David stood silently throughout. After a good deal more talk of this sort, during which no one changed anyone's mind in the slightest, Considére said he would have to consult with his associates, and would be back in a couple of hours. Frydman and Wegrow accepted this delay, and Considére, David and the valise departed.

For three or four hours, amid the ribbons, the flowers, the feathers and the dust, Frydman and Wegrow waited fretfully, to the great prejudice of the milliner's peace of mind and workroom stock. Frydman kept absent-mindedly picking his teeth with feathers, despite the proprietress's shrill and repeated protests, and Wegrow, always a nervous type, defoliated enough artificial shrubbery to ornament a gross of Easter bonnets. Presently Considére, David and the valise returned. The valise was evidently much easier for David to manage this time than on its first appearance. Considére announced that he had induced his collaborators to let Jake have a thousand of the cheques in consideration of the many happy hours he and Jake had spent together. Frydman and Wegrow were much too relieved at getting any cheques at all to quarrel with either the form or content of these remarks. They transferred the cheques from the valise to several of the milliner's hatboxes, and bid farewell, they hoped forever, to Considére. After all, one thousand cheques, even at the low wholesale rate of seventy-five francs to the dollar, represented seven and a half million francs, a fair return on an investment of three or four hundred thousand. (By the same reckoning, of course, the five thousand cheques Vignon kept, represented thirty-seven and a half million francs for no investment at all.)

4 *Traveling men*

At this point the plot assumed the tempo of a Mack Sennett chase sequence. Both Vignon and Jake were madly anxious to get the goods on the market before the other one did. The night of the delivery at the millinery shop, Frydman and Jake boarded a plane for Belgium, and on the 21st they were already spreading counterfeits around Brussels and Antwerp, whether for Palestine's sake in addition to their own is still an open question. That solitary cheque that appeared and then disappeared at the Brussels Bourse on the 24th was from their allotment; and so was the one that showed up in Lucerne the following week, and the seven in Basle in July. It was from Frydman himself that the fifty were confiscated at Vallorbe toward the end of July. On the whole, examination of the signatures on the cheques showed, most of the ones that appeared in the low countries, Scandinavia, Germany, Austria, Czechoslovakia and northern Switzerland came originally from Frydman and Jake, although it was impossible in any case to be sure just how. Several items from this allotment even turned up a good deal later in Caracas,

Venezuela, where they had arrived, somehow or other, from Czechoslovakia.

Vignon, meanwhile, was being anything but idle. At the very moment that David and Considére were in the millinery shop, Vignon was unloading cheques on the Paris black market in wholesale lots. He got a substantial number into the hands of the jobbers who supplied the airline pilot. (These jobbers subsequently attempted to avoid paying for the cheques, but Vignon was not to be trifled with in this fashion; he collected the money at the point of a pistol.) A hundred from his supply were, while Frydman and Jake were flying north, speeding south on a train, in the hands of four black market characters from Paris. They stopped at Lyon, where they got rid of twenty-five on the 21st and 22nd, then proceeded to Nice, where they were arrested with the other seventy-five. Still another hundred of Vignon's cheques found their way into the hands of the South American diplomat who deposited them in Geneva. Vignon had kept such an enormous number of the counterfeits, however, that he never was able to dispose of more than a small part. (Only eleven hundred-odd of the six thousand that were printed ever showed up.) He was arrested, with Guitard, on a balmy June day in 1948, while the two of them were fishing from a rowboat on a lake near Champigny. One report was that, a day or two after the arrest, his wife burned his remaining stock. Burned or not the police were never able to find it.

If the details of what became of Vignon's and Jake's cheques are vague, however, the story of how Chauvet and David disposed of the five hundred or so they were given as a commission is quite circumstantial. Among Parisian counterfeiters, the principal rival to Vignon's mob was a gang that congregated in another café. At the very time that Vignon was toiling in the cellar in Champigny, this crew had perfected an ambitious plan for bringing out a fifty-dollar counterfeit American Express traveler's cheque, to be followed by a twenty and then a ten. In pursuance of this scheme one of the gang's printers, a sparrow-like, black-toothed little chatterbox named Michel Pica, volunteered to locate a supply of paper. One of the first people he talked to was Chauvet, an old acquaintance. As per his reputation Chauvet, once he had consumed a couple of *fines,* proved a rewarding conversationalist. Pica was able to report back that a hundred-dollar cheque was already in the works. Pica's boss concluded, in a fit of inspired generalship, that it would be simpler, safer and cheaper to get hold of a batch of the hundreds than to make his own fifties. A few days later Pica looked up Chauvet again and told him that in view of the impending issue of the hundreds, his friends had dropped their manufacturing plans. But, he added, if Chauvet anticipated any difficulty in disposing of his cheques, perhaps they could help him out, since they knew a party who was willing to buy an almost unlimited amount. Chauvet and David, as a matter of fact, did anticipate some difficulty; it was the beginning of July by then; the American Express warning was out and the black market had turned cool to the cheques. Chauvet was enchanted with Pica's offer, and reported it to David. David, a considerably brighter fellow than his buddy, suspected something fishy and decided that Pica's friends ought to be interviewed before they were entrusted with any large quantity of cheques. Accordingly a rendezvous was made at a café called La Perrichonne, on the Boulevard Voltaire, at which Pica introduced Chauvet and Da-

vid to a pair of characters named Robert Frederick
Haerdter and Philippe Bisschot. David had brought along
eleven of the cheques as a preliminary allotment.

Bisschot was an unremarkable young Belgian ne'er-do-
well who traveled on his brother's passport because he had
sold his own during a personal fiscal crisis a couple of
years before, and whose only business asset was a certain
talent for crude mimicry, by the use of which he was able
to approximate the sleek appearance and fluent talk of a
traveling salesman. Haerdter, though, was something
rather special. He was a slender, middle-aged German
whose every aquiline lineament proclaimed him a gentleman. He was partly bald, in an aristocratic kind of way;
the clothes he wore were conscientiously tailored; his
manners blended courtesy with condescension in faultless
proportion; he spoke French grammatically and glibly,
and with just a well-bred shadow of a British accent, and
English as if he had left Oxford not twenty-four hours before. This last accomplishment had enabled him, on numerous occasions, to assume the personality of a mythical
Briton named George Henry Bell, the younger son of an
impoverished county family, for he was no post-war par-
venu in the counterfeiting trade. His first arrest for broad-
casting bogus money had occurred in 1917 in Copen-
hagen; he had been deported from England as a suspected
forger in the early thirties; the most recent entry in the
extensive dossiers that the police departments of half a
dozen countries kept on him had concerned his role in
supplying several members of the U. S. Army of Occupation in Germany with counterfeit dollars. Charming a
pair of mugs like Chauvet and David was not a very taxing
task for him. After examining the eleven specimens, he
told them that he and Bisschot were acting as middlemen

for a fellow who was anxious to acquire as many more of the cheques as were available—to be paid for, of course, upon delivery. Chauvet succumbed to his blandishments without a struggle, but David was made of slightly sterner material, and asked for some evidence of good faith. Haerdter, with a lordly gesture, produced his wallet—a monogrammed gold-cornered one—counted out eighty-eight thousand francs, to pay for eleven cheques at eighty francs to the dollar, and carelessly tossed the money to David. David's doubts evaporated without leaving a trace, and he promised to show up at the same place next morning with four hundred-odd cheques more.

The scene that took place at La Perrichonne next morning must certainly have been unique in the annals of that not very notable establishment. Chauvet and David arrived first, carrying a valise with the cheques inside. Then Pica came, alone. (He was most carefully keeping up the appearance of being a friend of both groups.) Finally Haerdter and Bisschot drove up in Bisschot's Citroen. They sat at a table, opened the suitcase, and spread out the cheques. Haerdter said that his customer insisted that all of them be signed and countersigned. It turned out that no one had a pen, so Pica went to the stationer's next door and borrowed an inkpot and four pens. At first David cautiously refused to have anything to do with this literary work, but he was finally induced to sign a few of them. For the next hour or two David hovered sulkily in the background, keeping an eye out for the police, while the other four wrote down Anglo-Saxon names as fast as they could, to Haerdter's dictation. Haerdter himself did more than half the signing, being the only thoroughly literate person present. Pica and Bisschot labored hard, but inefficiently, frequently moistening their pens with the tips of their tongues, and flexing their fingers to ward off writer's cramp. Chauvet spent most of his time drinking, and presently became so befuddled that he signed at least one of the cheques with his own name.

Once this singular chirographical exercise had been completed, the cheques were loaded back into the bag, and Pica, Haerdter, Bisschot and Chauvet, with the latter in charge of the cheques, piled into the Citroen. David, ever circumspect, declined to accompany them, but before they drove off he found an opportunity to privately enjoin Chauvet to keep a vigilant eye on the others. Bisschot parked the car several doors away from the Astoria Hotel on the Champs Elysées, which was U. S. Army headquarters and where the alleged customer was allegedly employed. Haerdter got out, announcing he would go inside first, without the valise, to see that everything was in good order. He was gone for a few minutes, then returned and declared that the coast was clear. Chauvet gave him the bag, and followed him into the hotel at a discreet distance. Bisschot also got out of the car and posted himself on a bench. Pica remained in the car. Chauvet followed Haerdter up to the third floor of the hotel. There, in the corridor, two men, obviously plainclothes detectives, stepped from the shadows, grasped Haerdter firmly by the arm, said, in effect, "Alors, Freddy, this time we got you with the goods, *n'est ce pas?*," and led him back downstairs and out of the hotel. Chauvet again followed, this time at an even discreeter distance. He reached the Champs Elysées just in time to see Haerdter and his escorts—and the valise—descending into a Métro station. Pica still sat in the car, quivering. Bisschot, on the bench, was weeping large tears and even pulling out an occasional handful of hair.

Bisschot's behavior was a triumph of tragic acting, since he was perfectly aware—having helped cook up the scheme—that one of the plainclothes detectives was an ex-police inspector named Dominique Talamoni, who had been unfrocked for black market operations a couple of years before, and who had since found employment as a general handyman for the Pica-Bisschot-Haerdter mob. (The other detective, furnished by Talamoni, was an inspector still on the force, but his role in this affair was quite unofficial, to say the least.) Haerdter's captors took him, of course, not to any police station, but to the café, where Bisschot presently joined them and a hearty laugh was had by all. Pica's job, meanwhile, was to stay close to Chauvet and David and see to it that no nasty, suspicious thoughts came into their heads. In David's case this was quite a project, but Pica managed it skillfully. Two or three days after the hijack he took Chauvet and David into the café, and presented the proprietor to them as a man who would be able to find out from official sources whether Haerdter had really been arrested. (At that very moment Haerdter was concealed in a room back of the bar.) The proprietor proved most obliging, and made a phone call, presumably to a friend of his at police headquarters. This friend, the proprietor told Chauvet and David, said that Haerdter was indeed in custody. Chauvet and David eventually found out what had really happened, but by the time they did it was too late. The cheques by then were circulating in half the countries of Europe. The thirty that the three men were caught with in Geneva, for example, had been bought from Haerdter and Bisschot, and in August Bisschot and Talamoni made an extensive tour of Italy, cashing the "Rinc" cheques. (On these, examination showed, the signatures that had been put on at La Perrichonne had been removed with eradicator, and Bisschot had then signed them with his own name.) Just what Pica got out of all this remains obscure. Perhaps the other three double-crossed him, too. That would account for his having been associated with Chauvet subsequently in a food stamp counterfeiting plot which was what led to his and Chauvet's arrest, and to their being connected with the traveler's cheques. Bisschot, who had been searched for ever since the "Rinc" signature was deciphered, was finally arrested in Paris in the process of attempting to sell counterfeit rare postage stamps to a dealer, and Haerdter was ultimately nabbed by army authorities in Germany with a fair number of phony dollars on his person.

The trial took place in March, 1950. Present, and convicted, in addition to hordes of small fry, were Benor, Bisschot, Chauvet, Considére, Guitard, Pica and Wegrow. Not present, but also convicted, were Haerdter, who was serving twelve years in Germany for the dollar offense; Frydman, who never had been located, despite a pan-European search that had been on for two and a half years (he was found at last, under a new name, in a D.P. camp in Italy, and is still fighting extradition to France); Jake, who was in New York and hence beyond the reach of the French law; and Hirscovics, who apparently was running a boardinghouse in Tel Aviv whence he was writing provocative letters to friends in Paris about the import of hams, a class of goods whose utility to either Jews or Arabs was, in the opinion of the police, questionable. Vignon was acquitted, but his liberty was not to endure for long. The one important unanswered question at the time of the trial was where and on what the cheques had been printed. A few months later the police uncovered the details about the Webendorfer and the cellar in Champigny and Vignon was returned to jail.

Meanwhile one of the counterfeits still turns up every so often, particularly on the French Riviera, and there is little doubt that many of the people who handled them at their prime are still at large. Livingston isn't fretting, though. He estimates that, however many of the peripheral characters remained undetected, just about all the central figures were brought to book, and he is content to be residing once more in the uncomplicated precincts of Summit, New Jersey.

PART FOUR

Jorge Gregorio Simonovich

1 *From Minsk to the Polaco*

Since professional criminals, no less than businessmen of the orthodox sort, are governed in their choice of the goods or services they supply by what the public demands, it was entirely natural that one lively branch of crime in the years just after the end of the Second World War should have been the smuggling of aliens into the United States of America. The combination of strict American immigration laws and hundreds of thousands of oppressed, displaced or merely discontented people all over the world whose need or desire to enter the United States far outweighed their scruples about how to do it created a particularly favorable climate for such queer journeymen as the passport-and-birth-certificate forger, the nefarious motor-launch skipper, the hare-brained private pilot, and, especially, that curious variety of travel agent who specializes in providing accommodations under bunches of bananas and who routes his clients via uninhabited coves and abandoned cow pastures. Even in a favorable climate, however, alien smuggling is a difficult and restricted trade, largely because of the peculiar geography of the United States. To the west and to the east are several thousand miles of uninterrupted ocean, too long a haul, for the most part, for bulky, highly perishable contraband like people. To the north and half of the south are long, wild, unguardable land borders across which any moderately resourceful hiking enthusiast can slip unobserved without help from a professional smuggler, as witness the eternal and almost insoluble problem of the Mexican wetbacks. It is only on the Gulf of Mexico and the East Coast of Florida, a stretch of shore that is easily reached by small craft, air or water, from the islands in the Caribbean, that a smuggler finds any real scope. In that area Havana, a city that has a big foreign-born population and unpredictable law enforcement and is only a little over two hundred air miles from Miami, has been the traditional point of departure for would-be illegal entrants ever since the United States gave up its policy of unrestricted immigration right after the end of the First World War. The exact number of aliens who enter the United States illegally during any particular period of time is obviously impossible to calculate accurately, but it seems probable that several thousand of them managed in one way or another to arrive in Florida from Cuba during the years from 1946 to 1951. Of these a substantial number, running into the hundreds, booked their passage through a mousy little Russian named Jorge Gregorio Simonovich, who was, as far as the United States Immigration and Naturalization Service can tell, the most successful alien smuggler ever to practice the profession.

However, the word "successful," when used to describe Simonovich's felonious career, must be qualified heavily. According to folk lore, a master criminal is a suave, thickly jeweled fellow who, during those hours when he isn't baffling the police, is either wading knee deep in oriental carpets or feeding champagne to the entire chorus line of the biggest hit on Broadway. Simonovich never trod an oriental carpet or bought champagne for a chorus girl in his life; he was a hard-working family man whose earnings were just about enough to maintain his wife and two sons in lower-middle-class comfort in a walk-up apartment on an obscure Havana side street. His favorite tipple was unsweetened black coffee, and his customary garb was sandals, dungarees and an open-necked blue work shirt. What's more, he never even baffled the police. His lawbreaking extended, at the very least, from early in 1947 until, in the most mysterious action he ever performed, he managed to get arrested on a deserted landing strip just outside Miami on November 4, 1951. During that entire period the United States Border Patrol, which is the uniformed police force maintained by the Immigration and Naturalization Service, knew all about him and what he was up to. By the time he was arrested he had been indicted by three separate federal grand juries, and numbers of his accomplices, principally desperate American aviators, had been caught, tried and convicted. He was able to pursue his unmysterious way for so long for the simple reason that he lived in Cuba, and the extradition treaty between Cuba and the United States does not include the smuggling of aliens as an extraditable offense. Master criminal or not, however, Simonovich was a highly troublesome operator as far as the Border Patrol was concerned. Despite his drab personality, he was responsible for a long series of as lurid events as the patrol ever had to cope with. And ever since his arrest, illegal immigration from Cuba, which during his heyday was one of the patrol's most vexing problems, has almost ceased to be a problem at all.

Silence, particularly in the face of official interrogation, is one of Simonovich's most marked qualities, so that the facts of his early life are on the whole obscure. He was born in 1905 in Minsk. His people, apparently, were fairly well-to-do landowners. He himself received a technical education, culminating in a school for future army officers. When he was eighteen he was commissioned a second lieutenant in the Red army and assigned to duty on the Rumanian border. He promptly walked across, spent a year or so in various European countries doing no one knows what, and arrived in Cuba in April of 1924. His entry was perfectly legal. He worked for a while as a mechanic in the city of Camaguey, then moved to Havana, where he started his own business as a window shade and Venetian blind expert. It was roughly in 1930, when the Venetian blind business, like most others, became precarious, that he first ventured into more questionable commercial areas. He began supplementing his income with an occasional flyer in the rum trade with the United States. He was able to gratify his taste for intrigue in this manner because the neighborhood in which he lived, Havana's Polaco—literally, Polish quarter—is among the globe's yeastiest districts. Although, as the name of the quarter implies, natives of Eastern Europe are to be found in profusion in the Polaco, so are natives of almost any other country on earth. Traditionally Cuba has made few difficulties for immigrants as far as actual entry is concerned. Its method of protecting the local citizenry from cheap foreign labor has been to make it difficult to get a work permit. Consequently, since Havana is an ideal place to sit and wait for a United States visa to come through, the city is always filled with an assortment of unemployed characters whose financial resources and ethics cover a very wide range indeed. These characters tend to congregate in the Polaco, where rents are cheap, compatriots are easy to find, and there is an exceptionally complete collection of saloons and coffee shops in which to while the time away. In an environment like that the inquiring mind of man is bound to dwell on such subjects as how to make a fast buck; frequently, in fact, man is impelled to test in action the conclusions reached by his inquiring mind. As an old Polaco hand Simonovich, even if he had tried, could not very well have avoided hearing about an occasional cabal. He certainly did not try.

From the time he first associated himself with lawbreaking Simonovich was consistently non-adventurous. He toted no tommy guns, and piloted no contraband-laden motor launches. As a matter of fact he invested no capital. His distinctive role was to sit in various public places, sipping endlessly on strong black coffee, and talk. He talked with people who had rum to sell, with people who had money with which to buy rum, with people who had conveyances in which to transport rum, and with people who had official positions which called for them to oversee the manufacture, sale and distribution of rum. With a persuasive show of reluctance, and only after being paid in cash, he introduced some of these people to each other, and suggested to them appropriate ways in which they could cooperate. It was a line of work for which he was admirably suited by both temperament and talent, or he could not have survived for more than a few months. No kind of criminal operative is in more continuous peril than the unarmed scrawny little middleman. Once he has introduced one ham-handed swashbuckler to another he is, as far as they are concerned, clearly supererogatory, and both prudence and penury demand that they eliminate him. Simonovich's equilibrium in that unsettling environment was truly brilliant. One thing he always made clear at the outset of negotiation was that he had carefully committed to paper, and left with a loyal friend, all the pertinent names, places, sums of money, and methods of operation involved, along with instructions that the document be turned over to the authorities in the event that anything untoward occurred. From the first the existence, genuine or feigned, of such written materials gave even his most ferocious business acquaintances pause, and as time passed the dossiers he was ostensibly accumulating grew so numerous and inclusive that he was able to use them for other purposes than mere personal security: for blackmail when business was bad, or for dissuading colleagues who were becoming impatient with him from transferring their trade to rival agents. A second line of defense that he set up simultaneously with the first was to systematically sell United States prohibition agents information about one out of every three or four or five of the shipments he knew about, thus serving the quadruple purpose of increasing his income, keeping the law at least partly on his side, undoing his competition, and ridding himself of partners who were becoming troublesome. It took enormous adroitness to perform these complicated evolutions, as Simonovich did, for twenty-one years without being molested. One is constrained to wonder why a man with such a flair for business found it necessary to go outside the law to make a small living. Perhaps it was because the flair was unique only there.

The repeal of prohibition made very little difference in Simonovich's way of life other than to change the merchandise with which he concerned himself from liquor to people, and in the Polaco people ready to be smuggled into the United States, particularly after the accession of Adolph Hitler, were certainly no harder to find than cases of rum in the same condition. Cuba, of course, has always been an excellent headquarters for smugglers. It is close enough to the Florida coast to make the trip between the two in a small boat fairly uneventful, and both Cuba and Florida have long, intricate shorelines which make it easy to operate small boats unobtrusively. By exercising ordinary prudence a smuggler working out of Cuba can expect to have a long and prosperous career. Simonovich, with his elaborate documents and his pleasant connections with United States prohibition men and, subsequently customs and immigration agents, exercised a prudence that was far from ordinary. On one occasion in the late thirties, apparently, he even made a quiet trip to New York under the auspices of the Immigration Service for the purpose of scouring Chinatown for a number of hapless aliens he had smuggled in a short time before. One quite uncorroborated rumor had it that he succeeded in finding most of them and, after extorting various sums of money from their families on the promise that he would not turn them over to the authorities, proceeded blithely to turn them over. If he actually did make such a trip, it was undoubtedly the most lurid event in his otherwise placid, coffee-sipping life during the thirties. In 1940, when the European war intensified the interest of the United States government in the question of who was getting into the country, Simonovich was put on a regular monthly retainer of perhaps a hundred and fifty dollars or so by the Immigration Service, and continued to draw it through the war and until 1947 when balancing the budget became an issue again, and, very likely, Washington no longer thought the international situation was so tense that it justified subsidizing characters as questionable as Simonovich. That was when his troubles started.

Being stricken from the payroll after his many years of faithful service filled Simonovich with rancor. It also placed him in a painful economic quandary, not especially because of the lost wages but because of the greatly magnified peril of transacting business in the teeth of the Immigration Service's Border Patrol, a skillful and efficient police force to which he was not precisely a stranger. It is possible that Simonovich, at that point, would have returned to Venetian blinds if he had been able to. However the Cuban Government, nonchalant as it had been about Simonovich's way of life, had not been so bland as to allow him citizenship or even a work permit. He had married, in the early thirties, a Polish-born Cuban citizen named Berta Dembrowska, and was the father of two boys approaching their teens. As an affectionate and responsible breadwinner he had no alternative but to continue a life of crime, and it didn't take him long to find an admirable collaborator in the person of Edward William Murphy of Sioux City, Iowa.

2 *From Sioux City to Teterboro to jail*

In both appearance and character Murphy bore as little resemblance to Simonovich as one crook is ever likely to bear to another. He was an aviator straight out of folklore: tall, strong, handsome and courageous; a veteran barnstormer whose formidable technique as a flyer filled his fellow practitioners with awe, and whose long pre-war police record, which included arrests in several cities for grand larceny, breaking and entering, and interfering with an election, made it impossible for him to get steady commercial work—assuming he would have consented to occupy himself with anything that tepid. During the war Murphy had worked for the army as a civilian, first as a flight instructor, then as a ferry pilot—which hadn't prevented him from being convicted of grand larceny in Miami in 1942 for stealing the tires of a rented car. His sentence, presumably because of his useful war work, was deferred. After the war he busied himself with various odd flying jobs involving small planes, and finally wound up in the pay of some insurrectionary Dominicans who were anxious to unseat Rafael Trujillo as president of their native land. His part in this cabal was to move down to Cuba, where the plot was being brewed, and teach various plotters to fly. There is reason to believe that he was also under contract, when the time came, to sneak some of them into the Dominican Republic, but the entire affair disintegrated before he ever had occasion to execute any such stimulating maneuvers. He had to content himself with ferrying them quietly back to Florida —most of them were U. S. citizens—when the plot collapsed. It was as this job was coming to a close, and it was necessary for him to search for new employment, that he met Simonovich in Havana. It was a pleasurable encounter for Murphy; as is often the case, the financial temptations of private industry were substantially greater than those of politics. Peripatetic Dominicans were worth only seventy-five or a hundred dollars each to Murphy, whereas Simonovich's clientele was at least two or three times that openhanded. For Simonovich, too, his new acquaintance was a joy. In alien smuggling, as in many other branches of the shipping trade, the air age had arrived, and Murphy was not only an excellent pilot, but one with peculiar knowledge of how to run unnoticed between the United States and Cuba. Only one discord jarred the harmony of this relationship. Murphy had been presented to Simonovich by one Verdugo Ramírez, a Cuban felon-of-all-work who had been mixed up in the Dominican plot—every underground movement benefits by a bit of professional criminal assistance. Not only did Ramírez have to be cut in, but so did several friends whom he had also brought into the scheme. Ramírez, apparently, was a stickler for correct organization, and insisted on having on hand a cooperating airfield owner at twenty percent of the profits; a government fixer at fifteen percent; a Miami resident, responsible for carrying the merchandise north, at fifteen percent, and, of course, himself, as coordinator, at fifteen percent. All these costly and, from the point of view of Murphy and Simonovich, clearly nonessential, characters left the two of them with just thirty-five percent between them. The list price for passage was to be one thousand dollars for a European, fifteen hundred for a Chinese, but of course all expenses had to come out of that: gasoline for the plane, transportation from Florida north, grease for whatever Cuban officials needed it, and so forth. Under the circumstances Murphy, who was getting twenty percent, could hope to make at best two hundred dollars a Chinese, and Simonovich who was getting fifteen, one hundred and fifty. As a matter of fact, nine times out of ten they couldn't hope to realize that much. Alien smuggling is strictly a Collect on Delivery business, and if a smuggler, having taken a Chinese clear from the outskirts of Havana to the arms of his loving uncle on Mott Street at a contract price of fifteen hundred dollars, is then told by that uncle that eleven hundred dollars is all he is going to get, the smuggler is very unlikely to refuse the money and carry the passenger back to Havana.

Murphy's first flight to Florida, as far as the Border Patrol knows, was on November 11, 1947. He carried two European refugees, both with Auschwitz numbers tattooed on their arms, as well as Ramírez, who was going to Florida to see that the American end of the business was running properly. The flight left from Santa Fe Airport, a little landing field about fourteen miles out of Havana, and landed at an equally obscure field near Miami. (During the war Florida had been a major Air Force training center, and literally hundreds of fields, many of them little more than concrete strips out in the bushes, had been installed there. There was never any problem about finding an inconspicuous place to land a plane in Florida.) Simonovich was present at Santa Fe to witness the takeoff. Before boarding the plane one of the refugees, tears streaming from his eyes, kissed him on both cheeks. The same man, when he alighted in Florida, kissed the ground. Each of the refugees paid Ramírez six hundred dollars upon arrival. The crossing was completely uneventful. Murphy's next trip, equally painless, was on November 28, when he carried a wealthy South American lady in solitary splendor. She paid in advance. Those first two flights boded so well for the future of the syndicate that, before another trip was made, Murphy's little open-cockpit BT-13 was replaced by a six-passenger cabin job. On December 10 the new plane was put into operation, carrying Chinese—three of them—for the first time, as well as Ramírez and Simonovich himself. Ramírez took the Chinese to New York, where he was paid for them. As for Simonovich's journey, it was the result of some extremely confidential conversations between Murphy and himself. Now that a larger plane had been bought, and the general practicability of air transport established, the two men agreed Ramírez and his friends were no longer essential to the operation. Simonovich's excursion, ostensibly to share the responsibility and risk on the first trip with Chinese, was actually for the purpose of finding out whether the Florida end of the business could be handled without the assistance of Ramírez's representative there. This specimen was an all-around plug-ugly named Victor Frederico Guerrero Velasquez and called Freddy, who in the course of an eventful life had done time as a Miami Beach butler and consequently was familiar with many of the byways of that devious city.

While Freddy accompanied Ramírez and the Chinese north and collected the passage money there, Simonovich and Murphy perfected plans for foiling him the next trip in. They executed these plans on December 17, with Simonovich safely back in Cuba, when Murphy carried in two more Chinese, whom he flew all the way to New York, personally collecting twelve hundred dollars for one and eleven hundred for the other. His passenger list was that small because, as a measure of common prudence, he had also carried to Florida his wife and two daughters. He didn't want them left in Cuba where Ramírez could wreak vengeance on them if he discovered the double cross. He did discover it too, tipped off by an airport employee who had observed the surreptitious departure of the Murphy ménage.

Neither Ramírez nor Freddy had any moral scruples about making their colleagues pay the traditional price for treason, but it was not sound business to do so. No other pilot with Murphy's qualifications was handy, and Simonovich's unique sources of supply plus the elaborately documented dossiers on his fellow conspirators to which he constantly alluded, made him indispensable too. Ramírez had to content himself with bellowing at Simonovich, which Simonovich endured with an admirable show of humility and repentance. Murphy had remained in Florida to settle his domestic affairs, and Freddy called upon him there. Murphy had already received a letter from Simonovich notifying him of what had occurred and instructing him how to behave, and so he too, by a considerable effort of will, acted meek, and agreed to accompany Freddy back to Cuba to pick up another load for the syndicate. He made it clear, though, that this was to be his last trip. He and his family, he told Ramírez and company, were now comfortably settled in Miami; he had sufficient cash to tide him over for a while, and prospects for making a living less perilously were good. He made his "last" run, carrying three Chinese, on January 2, 1948. Freddy, who went along as supercargo, took the passengers north. No sooner had Freddy turned his back than Murphy, leaving his own plane at Tropicaire airport near Miami, quietly rented a smaller plane at another airfield and returned to Cuba where Simonovich had lined up two more non-syndicate passengers, a European and a Chinese. This flight took off from a Cuban pasture on January 7, and went all the way to Teterboro Airport. On January 8 Murphy delivered the European to relatives in Brooklyn and was paid five hundred dollars. (Simonovich had already received a two-hundred-dollar down payment on this passage in Havana.) On January 9 the Chinese was handed over to friends in Cranford, New Jersey, for fifteen hundred dollars.

With his share of this money, Murphy bought a trailer, which he parked near Tropicaire, and moved out of the house of his wife's mother in Miami, where he had been temporarily putting up. For more than six weeks he led an exemplary life, making what money he could by chartering his plane and giving private flying lessions. Although his purpose in thus suspending activities was to frustrate whatever bloodthirsty plans Ramírez and Freddy might cook up if they found that he had really not retired, the blameless life he led for those six weeks actually bothered the Border Patrol more than it did his ex-colleagues. Toward the beginning of January the patrol had gotten hold of a copy of the warning letter Simonovich had sent Murphy after their first private endeavor, and had, with little trouble, found where and who Murphy was. (Where and who Simonovich was the patrol had known for a long time.) Neither the terms of Simonovich's letter, which were oblique, nor the patrol's scanty supply of manpower, justified a twenty-four-hour watch on Murphy. All the patrol could do was to check into his background, keep an occasional eye on him, and warn airport employees all over Florida to report at once anything that looked even faintly suspicious. If Murphy had been doing business at his December rate he undoubtedly would have been caught right then. He didn't make a move, though, between January 8 and February 22. On that date, again in a rented plane, again using a Cuban pasture rather than an airport, he took off with one European and three Chinese whom Simonovich had booked. His first stop was Miami, where the European was delivered to an uncle for six hundred dollars. Then the flight proceeded north to Baltimore, where one Chinese was dropped off upon receipt of fourteen hundred, on to New York, where the second Chinese brought in fifteen hundred, and finally to Chicago, where the third was worth fourteen hundred again. It was a lucrative trip, and it was managed without the knowledge of either Ramírez or the Border Patrol.

After this coup Murphy and Simonovich again exercised prudence and lay low for several weeks. Then, on March 14, they arranged another flight, with five Chinese aboard this time, and again they brought it off successfully. Their next departure they scheduled a mere two weeks later, on Easter Sunday, calculating no doubt that most members of the Border Patrol would be exhibiting new hats that day instead of working. This calculation was not up to their usual canny standard. At about five in the afternoon, Murphy, flying a twin-engined red

Cessna with five Chinese aboard, put down for fuel at the small airport in Fernandina, Florida, near Jacksonville. As the airport manager was filling the tanks, one of the passengers tried to get out. Murphy curtly ordered him to stay inside. The airport manager was an alert young man who had received the Border Patrol's circular asking for a report on any odd events he might observe; Murphy's attitude toward his passengers appeared extremely odd. When Murphy went off to the airport's refreshment stand to get crackers and pop for himself and his passengers, the manager sneaked a quick look into the plane's cabin. Although it was pretty murky in there and the passengers were well bundled up, he was sure he saw yellow skin and slanted eyes. Murphy came back and paid him for the gas. The thick roll of bills he produced in so doing contributed to the manager's distrust. When the plane took off, heading north, he called the patrol's Jacksonville office and reported what had happened. The Patrol promptly asked the Civil Aeronautics Authority to keep track of the plane and to check its ownership. The CAA first was able to report that the plane was registered in the name of a Florida dealer, and second, that it had landed after dark at Raleigh, North Carolina; had taken off again at about dawn on Monday, and had landed at Teterboro in the middle of the morning. At Teterboro a car had been waiting for the plane in a far corner of the field, and the passengers had been rapidly transferred into it and driven away, where to no one was able to say. The dealer, upon being questioned, said that he had just sold the plane to one Edward William Murphy. At this point the Border Patrol's previous research into Murphy's life more than justified itself. One apparently minor fact that had been entered in the files was that on a former trip to New York Murphy had stayed at the National Hotel. A check with the manager showed that he was again registered there, together with his wife and a man suggestively named Tom Moy. If the patrol could have been sure that Tom Moy was an illegal immigrant—which he was—Murphy would have been arrested then and there, but there was always the possibility that Moy had every right to be in the United States, in which case an arrest would serve no purpose except allowing the conspirators to cover up. The patrol decided to wait.

Moy was Chicago bound. Murphy had delivered his four other passengers to Chinatown for forty-nine hundred dollars, while the patrol was discovering that he was the plane's owner, and locating him at the National. When he went out to Teterboro to arrange for the last leg of his flight, the patrol finally had him in continuous view. At Teterboro a couple of men representing themselves as CAA officials said they wanted to ask him some routine questions. The questions they asked, though, struck Murphy as being of a peculiarly non-CAA type. He became alarmed, and hastily changed his plans. Hurrying back to the hotel, he picked up Moy, took him to a bus depot and sent him off to Chicago that way. Then he returned to Teterboro with his wife and took off for, he said, Washington. They never showed up in Washington, but landed at a tiny strip in South Carolina, where Murphy put the plane into storage. Then they went back to Miami, packed their belongings, hooked up the trailer and headed for Iowa, Murphy's ancestral home. One thing the patrol did not want was for Murphy, once he was back in it, to leave the Dade County jurisdiction where that wartime sentence for tire stealing was still hanging over him. And so he was brought in before he was able to get over the county line.

When first questioned by the Border Patrol Murphy was by no means garrulous, but once he had been given time to think over his position, with special reference to the deferred grand larceny sentence, he became so. He enumerated his several flights, mentioned Simonovich, Ramírez, Freddy and the other conspirators and, finally, spent a couple of weeks with a patrol inspector touring the country and unearthing various of the aliens he had brought in. The wheels of justice grind no more rapidly in Florida than anywhere else. Murphy was arrested on April 5, 1948. It wasn't until October 22 that a federal grand jury got around to indicting him, Simonovich, Freddy, Ramírez and thirteen others, including ten of the aliens that had been smuggled in. Murphy and Freddy—the only two of the conspirators that could be found—were arraigned on January 7, 1949, and pleaded guilty. They each were sentenced to two years in prison on August 12. After a suitable lapse of time the prosecution of the ten aliens was dropped, and the indictment against Simonovich was also allowed to lapse after he had been sent up on various other counts. The indictments against Ramírez and three of his friends still stand and will doubtless be pushed if and when they ever come within reach of the United States courts, an unlikely possibility at best.

While Murphy was thus being dissected north of the border, Simonovich, south of it, continued unperturbed on his daily rounds. Through a representative attached to the American Embassy in Havana, the Border Patrol kept as close a check on him as it could. There was every reason to believe that Murphy's capture merely caused Simonovich temporary inconvenience without in any way altering either his intentions or his deeds, but for nine months no evidence could be turned up that would establish the justice of this belief. Finally, early in the morning of January 9, 1949, a tip was received that Simonovich was being exceptionally active in the general neighborhood of the waterfront. Investigation disclosed that the vessel in which Simonovich was interested was a small lighter, apparently loaded with bananas, which chugged out of the harbor at about 7:30 A.M., and returned, still full of bananas, an hour or so later. The inference immediately drawn by the Border Patrol, of course, was that the lighter had met another boat just outside the harbor on an errand whose nature had very little to do with fruit. This was an opportunity for the patrol's heavy equipment to be put to work.

When the Miami office was apprised of the facts, it ordered all the radio cars available to proceed to the Keys and patrol them, and it sent its Grumman Widgeon amphibian patrol plane out over the Dry Tortugas to discover whether any boats that might have left Havana around eight A.M. were heading for Florida. The plane did locate such a boat that afternoon, and was able to report it as a two-masted fishing schooner, about forty-five feet long, equipped with an auxiliary motor that apparently gave it a speed of some six knots. It seemed to be headed for some place about halfway between Key Largo and Key West. The plane kept the boat in sight until dark, and at dawn it was in the air again. By then the boat was just off South Pigeon Key, heading toward the village of Marathon, on the end of Boot Key. By radio the men in the plane notified the men in the cars, and the cars converged on Marathon. When the boat, whose name turned out to be *Semper Fidelis,* pulled into a Marathon dock, there were Border Patrol men there to greet it in sufficient numbers to capture a small battleship. Aboard the *Semper Fidelis,* sure enough, were three illegal immigrants, a young Rumanian couple and a twenty-five-year-old Pole. All three were tattooed with concentration camp serial numbers, and bore on their persons such telltale marks as missing teeth, bayonet scars and badly set bones. The Rumanians had been in Buchenwald, the Pole in four different camps, including Auschwitz. Simonovich had received a total of twenty-six hundred dollars for their passage, practically all of it raised from relatives in New York, where they were bound. The crew of the *Semper Fidelis* was arrested immediately, of course. It consisted of the captain, Albert E. Padags of Marathon, a suspected smuggler for some time, who had chartered the boat from its Miami owner for $175 a week, ostensibly as a fishing boat, and two assistants named Joseph Sowinski and Arthur J. Benson. They were indicted on March 11, along with Simonovich, arraigned on April 1, and sentenced, upon pleas of guilty, on June 17. Padags got three years in prison and a fifteen hundred dollar fine. Benson and Sowinski were each put on probation for three years. The three refugees were given suspended sentences and permitted to stay in the country. Meanwhile, in Havana, Simonovich continued sipping coffee, not blithely, perhaps, but busily.

As the *Semper Fidelis* case was wending its way through the courts, a new, if minor, facet of Simonovich's profession was coming to light. On May 28 there arrived at International Airport, Miami, from Camaguey, Cuba, a heavy-set man with a thick Hungarian accent, bearing a birth certificate that identified him as George Bunting Little of Norfolk, Virginia. To the immigration inspectors at International Airport, who are accustomed to most forms of chicanery, he didn't look like any plausible George Bunting Little. It took only perfunctory questioning, in fact, to establish that he was Joseph Buday, a forty-five-year-old Hungarian tailor. A few hours later that same day a plane from Havana landed at the same airport carrying among its passengers an American school teacher named Anna Rohrbeck, who had been teaching English in Cuba, accompanied by a ten-year-old boy whom she identified as her son. Once again routine questioning by the immigration people elicited an amended, and considerably more truthful, statement of the facts. The boy turned out to be Franz Buday, Joseph's son. It appeared that the two Budays, after a series of dreadful wartime experiences that had left them, finally, the only surviving members of their family, had arrived in Cuba from England a year or

so before, with the hope that from there they could somehow get into the United States. Doing so legally had
proved to be a much more difficult proposition than Buday
had anticipated. Meanwhile he had met Simonovich at
one Polaco coffee house or another, and Simonovich had
offered to help him out for a consideration of seven hundred dollars. Buday didn't have seven hundred dollars,
and besides, even though his years with the Nazis were
not designed to inspire him with any affection for authority, he was fundamentally a law-abiding man. After he
had been in Cuba for six months or so and had substantially depleted such funds as he had, he met Mrs. Rohrbeck at the home of mutual acquaintances. Mrs. Rohrbeck
was much moved by the Budays' account of what they
had been through, and was particularly attracted by
young Franz who, she felt, was much the kind of a boy
her son might have become if he had lived. A warm friendship arose between them, and the teacher presently resolved that it was her duty to help the Budays. She offered
to bring Franz in as her son, if his father could find some
way to arrange his own passage. Throughout this time
Buday had been running across Simonovich around town,
and Simonovich had continued to try to peddle his wares.
When Mrs. Rohrbeck made her offer, Buday at last succumbed to Simonovich's blandishments and agreed to buy
the George Bunting Little birth certificate from him for
forty dollars. Where Simonovich got the certificate no one
ever found out for certain. The Border Patrol's guess was
that he had picked it up from a financially embarrassed
sailor who had jumped ship in Cuba. When they were
picked up in Miami, neither Buday nor Mrs. Rohrbeck
made any bones about what they had been up to, and the
authorities, in view of the strong mitigating circumstances,

were not inclined to be vindictive. Mrs. Rohrbeck was given a three-year probation, and so was the elder Buday. The Budays were returned to Cuba, whence, a few months later, they were allowed to enter the United States legally. And one more item was entered in the dossier on Simonovich, which was beginning to be bulky.

4 *The boys from Grand Rapids*

Buday's case was finally disposed of during October, 1949, by which time Simonovich was once again in full bloom. His associates this time were Gaylord Miles Saxton and Charles Cramton, a couple of young fliers from Grand Rapids, Michigan. Cramton was an amiable enough, not too bright, remarkably docile youth, but, as a Border Patrol inspector was to put it later, "If you think this Murphy was a desperate character, boy, you should of got a load of this Saxton." Saxton, a good-looking, strongly built, curly-headed infant of twenty-seven had, in his day, attended Michigan State College, from which he had failed to graduate, and Air Corps cadet school, from which he had failed to receive a commission. From 1940 to 1942 he was with the RAF in Canada as an instructor. (He was universally regarded as a superb, if maniacal flyer; his problem wherever he went was not skill but deportment.) In 1943 he settled in Miami, where he made a living for a while as a free-lance flyer. Then, after the war had ended and he had performed a number of laughable pranks like flying under clothes lines on Monday mornings and buzzing school playgrounds at recess time, his pilot's license was revoked by the Civil Aeronautics Authority. He was married by that time, and he turned to radio and television repair as a living, though it was hardly a stimulating one for a man of his moods. In the late summer of 1949, according to his own version of what happened, he read an article about Simonovich and Murphy in a national magazine. There, described in clear detail, was the life for him. On September 1 he took a commercial plane to Havana, went to the Polaco, and soon enough found Simonovich, just as the magazine had said he could. Two or three days later he returned home with all his problems solved except the relevant one of getting hold of a usable private pilot's license. He wasn't baffled for long. Cramton, an old high school and Miami friend and fellow mechanic, was presently at loose ends in Michigan, where he had been unloading the family farm following the death of his father. Not being nearly so dashing a blade as Saxton, he had managed to keep his pilot's license. Saxton wrote him asking to borrow it. In reply, Cramton nonchalantly forwarded the license together with a query about current employment conditions in Miami. Saxton wrote back that he was sure that he could find a way to move some cash in Cramton's direction.

Cramton promptly bought a new car on time, pledging himself to meet monthly payments of eighty-two dollars, and set out for Miami with his wife. He arrived on September 29 and, the following morning, checked in at Saxton's apartment. Mrs. Saxton greeted him with word that her husband had left a few hours before on a fast business trip to Cuba, from which he was scheduled to return during the afternoon. She asked Cramton to join her in meeting Saxton at Opa Locka airport then. Saxton landed on schedule in a Piper Clipper he had rented in Cramton's

name. With him was a young Rumanian woman. Cramton
drove the car right up to the plane, which had taxied to an
inconspicuous corner of the field, and the young woman
hastily transferred from one vehicle to the other. With the
Saxtons showing him the way, Cramton then drove to a
small hotel in a Miami suburb. Saxton and the young
woman went inside, and Saxton presently came out alone.
On the way back to his house he gave Cramton two hundred dollars. He also explained to Cramton what was going on. The young woman, he said, was the fifth member
of her family he had flown in from Cuba. Two weeks before he had brought in the other four, her older brother,
his wife and their two small children. Simonovich had
made the arrangements with still another brother, an elec-
rical engineer who was a Cuban citizen. Although this
was only the second flight, Saxton was well pleased with
the arrangements, which seemed to him quite foolproof.
His landing field in Cuba was a deserted stretch of beach
near the town of Cardenas, about four hours' drive from
Havana. Simonovich would take the passengers out there
by car, hide them in a handy nearby graveyard until he
saw the plane land, then rush them across the sand into
the plane. The whole procedure took no more than ten or
fifteen minutes, including refueling the plane. With a
choice of some three dozen obscure landing fields in
southern Florida to put down at, Saxton didn't see how in
the world he could ever be caught, particularly if someone
were always at hand at the chosen field to warn him off if
any police-like looking people were about, and to whisk
the passengers away if there weren't. It all seemed terribly
sensible to Cramton too.

Through October and November things went just as
smoothly as Saxton had imagined they would. Simonovich

had apparently struck a rich Rumanian vein in Havana. To the Border Patrol's positive (subsequent) knowledge, Saxton during that time made seven additional flights to Cuba and carried a total of twenty-four passengers. There is no reason to believe, either, that he didn't make several more trips that escaped official notice. With a volume of business that great, the profits were handsome. Saxton and Simonovich split fifty-fifty after expenses had been paid, which meant that during those two months each of them must have earned between four and five thousand dollars at least, more money than Saxton, even after paying the installments on Cramton's car, treating him and his wife to a weekend in Cuba, underwriting his grocery bills, and giving him frequent doses of cash, had ever seen. Not only did Saxton achieve prosperity but, apparently, contentment as well. He had found work in which he could take an honest pride, and he began to ornament it with those exuberant flourishes that distinguish the master craftsman from the mere journeyman. On the way up from Cuba he conscientiously used those intervals when managing the plane did not require his full attention to instruct his passengers in the manners and customs of the land they were about to enter. Hotel bellboys, he informed them, expected money in return for operating three light switches, pulling up two shades and opening one closet door. A large piece of ice in a glass of drinking water was a phenomenon that must be accepted calmly. On airplanes there were young women called stewardesses who were constantly offering a person chewing gum. After landing in Florida, where he would be met by his wife, Cramton and, frequently, Mrs. Cramton as well, he would continue to be helpful. If the passengers were going north, he would arrange their transportation, and on two or three occasions, when there was some delay in finding reservations, he put them up at his house for a day or two. He introduced them to cafeterias and counter joints, and told them how to avoid the look of the greenhorn by the offhand use of such terms as "Danish" and "Western on rye." Sometimes he purchased small items of wearing apparel for customers whose garb was too clearly alien, or luggage for those whose belongings were tied in a bundle. He was absolutely intransigent in forbidding head kerchiefs for women. One of his passengers, New York bound, had a small nondescript dog as her boon companion. When shipping difficulties arose and the lady became all but distracted, Saxton purchased some lumber and constructed a neat crate that solved the problem.

However, the Immigration Service is not a group that permits this sort of blissful existence to continue forever. Its routine procedures are carefully designed to frustrate any long-term large-scale conspiracy like the Simonovich-Saxton one. One part of those procedures is to keep an eye on potential illegal entrants in such cities as Havana. Most aliens anxious to enter the United States exhaust the legal possibilities before taking up with cruise directors like Simonovich, and so their names and addresses, as well as the names and addresses of friends or relatives in the United States, are easily found in the files of the appropriate U. S. consulate. Therefore, late in November, when it came to the attention of the Immigration Service people in Havana that a young Rumanian brother and sister had unaccountably vanished several days before, the wheels started turning. A check of the pair's visa applications at the consulate turned up a name and address in New York. The New York office of the Immigration Service was notified, and the building at that address was put under watch.

Only a day or two later a young couple answering to the Rumanians' description showed up there. They were unable to account for their presence in New York satisfactorily, and were invited to the Immigration Service office for questioning. If they are neither professional politicals nor professional crooks, illegal entrants caught in the act seldom hesitate to tell all to the police. This couple was no exception. They admitted they had flown in from Cuba to Florida, described the plane, the pilot, the landing field and all the details of their experience. When shown photographs of several known or suspected Cuban travel agents, they unhesitatingly picked Simonovich's as being a faithful likeness of the fellow they did business with.

To that point, of course, the police work had been fairly easy and not especially rewarding. It was scarcely news to the Immigration Service, after all, that Simonovich was smuggling aliens into the United States, and there wasn't much that could be done about him anyway. There was a chance, though, that the Rumanians might lead the way to Simonovich's American associates, and so the couple was sent down to Miami, turned over to the Border Patrol there, and taken on an exhaustive tour of nearby flying fields. On the fifth day, having examined a couple of dozen unfamiliar fields, the Rumanians were at last escorted to Opa Locka. They not only recognized it, but even were able to point to a small hotel close to it at which they had spent a night. From that moment on cracking the Saxton case was downhill work for the Border Patrol. The hotel manager, an observant and forthcoming type, remembered the Rumanians, remembered that they had been accompanied by two young Americans, one, apparently, a flyer, remembered that the flyer's appearance coincided closely with the Rumanians' description of their pilot, and even was able to produce an appropriately dated page of the hotel register on which the names of the Americans were clearly set forth as Gaylord Saxton and Charles Cramton. Meanwhile other mysterious disappearances from Havana's refugee colony were being investigated by the Immigration Service in Cleveland, Miami and New York, and eight more aliens were turned up who positively identified photographs of Simonovich and Saxton. Checking the dates given by these people, the patrol in Miami was able to determine that on each one of them Cramton had rented a plane at some airfield. A survey of Saxton's history had already disclosed his licenseless status. Arresting Saxton and Cramton at this juncture did not strike the patrol as an over-ambitious act, and on December 6, just nine days after the Rumanians had landed in Florida, the deed was done. The case against them was made even tidier, if it needed to be, when the patrol found in Saxton's pockets, when he was arrested, receipts for many of the planes Cramton had rented. Saxton and Cramton must have shared the patrol's view of the potency of the evidence, for they promptly dictated lengthy confessions. Saxton's alone took up some thirty typewritten pages, and included numerous names and telephone numbers which led to the discovery of most of the rest of his passengers. On February 27, 1950, Saxton and Cramton, their wives, Simonovich, and four relatives of the smuggled aliens were indicted on seven counts. On March 3 they all pleaded guilty except, of course, Simonovich, who remained placidly in Havana.

If, at this point, the Border Patrol was under the impression that its troubles with Saxton were over, it was about to be startled. At the beginning of April, when he and the other defendants were out on bail awaiting sentence early in May, he became fatigued with his sedentary life. He had somehow managed to maintain communications with Simonovich and had learned of a particularly lucrative job, involving two Chinese, that Simonovich had lined up. One morning he and Cramton calmly went out to Tamiami airport, talked the people there into renting them a Cessna 140 and an Ercoupe, despite the fact they had no licenses—Cramton's, of course, had been lifted after his arrest—and took off for Cuba. Within a few hours of their departure the Patrol, naturally, discovered that they were gone and in what direction. Their houses were put under watch, as well as all the likely airports around Miami—just because they had left from Tamiami didn't mean they were planning to return there—and the Widgeon was once again sent into the air to scout that part of the ocean which the pair was bound to traverse on their way back. As darkness fell, with no sign of the missing men, the weather turned stormy. A Cessna 140 is a two-passenger, short-range plane of exceptionally low power. An Ercoupe is no bigger and only slightly more powerful. To fly planes of this kind from Miami to Cuba in perfect weather is a rash act. The patrol pilot was positive that no one would be such an idiot as to do it at night in a storm, and besides his visibility was approaching zero and his gas was low. He put down for the night. The men at Saxton's and Cramton's houses, and at the airports, maintained their watch, however. At about midnight, with the rain coming down in sheets, a taxi pulled up to Saxton's door and Saxton stepped out into the arms of the patrol. He was perfectly cheerful when he saw the reception committee, said certainly he'd been in Cuba, and volunteered to show the patrol men what he'd been up to. The watch staked out at Cramton's home had picked their man up in a similar manner, meanwhile, and Cramton, too, had expressed his willingness to tell all. The two posses joined forces in a couple of Border Patrol cars, and Saxton directed them through the storm north of the city to an obscure dirt road. He climbed out of the car, firmly grasped by patrol officers, and whistled three times. Out of the bushes came a pair of puzzled looking, and extremely wet, Chinese. They were added to the caravan. Saxton then explained, with a good deal of pride, how he and Cramton had found that narrow road in the midst of a downpour, had performed the maniacal feat of landing on it, had let off their passengers, had then, even more maniacally, taken off again and brought their planes to Opa Locka, and were just about to change into dry clothes, pick up their cars and extricate the Chinese from the bushes when they were so rudely interrupted. Thoroughly astonished by this tale, the Border Patrol people, next day, checked the width of the road against a 140's wingspread. Sure enough, there was a foot or two of clearance on each side, and there were also the marks of plane tires in the mud to confirm the story.

From then until the date of sentence, May 7, the Border Patrol kept a closer eye on Saxton than it ordinarily does on a man who has pleaded guilty and who stands to lose a thousand dollars bail if he misbehaves. He attempted no more feats of strength or skill until the very last moment. At 10 A.M. on May 7, however, Mrs. Saxton, and Cramton and his wife showed up promptly at the United States Court House without Saxton but with a remarkable story. All four had been on their way to court a few minutes before, with Saxton driving, when he suddenly stopped the car, got out, said, "It's much too nice a day to go to jail," and walked away. The Border Patrol and the Federal Bureau of Investigation, which is the agency responsible for rounding up escaped federal prisoners, used about fifteen men and two weeks to find him. Finally a Border Patrol inspector got a tip that he was hiding out in a lonely house in the Everglades. He went out there just after dark one night, crept up to a lighted window on his belly, peered in and saw Saxton reclining peacefully on a couch reading a detective magazine. All Saxton said when the inspector walked in was, "How the hell did you ever find me here?" There was a .38 automatic under the pillow he was lying on—Saxton generally carried a gun—but he made no attempt to use it. He came quietly. The house was occupied by an elderly woman to whom Saxton had represented himself as an unemployed house painter in search of peace and quiet. He offered to paint the house, inside and out, in return for room and board. The job was almost finished when the Border Patrol caught up with him. Saxton received an eight-year sentence for his misdeeds, and lost half his bail. Cramton got five years, and the two wives got three years each, but their sentences were suspended.

5 *Too many informers; too few crooks*

Although disposing of Saxton and Cramton was gratifying, it made Simonovich no more accessible than ever, and the Border Patrol looked forward confidently to going another round with him and his friends. Its confidence was thoroughly justified. In the fall of 1950 a second national magazine ran an article on Simonovich, giving most of the details of the Saxton case, and the piece came to the attention of a couple of Hammond, Indiana, flyers named John Morgan and Marion N. Robinson. Just as Saxton had before them, they figured that no one so far had worked the racket with sufficient intelligence, and off they went to Havana to talk to Simonovich. As a result of this meeting they were able, on Christmas night, to fly four Chinese from Cuba to Fort Lauderdale, where they rented a station wagon and proceeded, unmolested, to New York. They got twenty-six hundred dollars for the job, about a thousand of which was their half of the profit, and felt that their original estimate of their talents was turning out to be quite accurate. On January 28—they weren't going to be in a hurry to get rich like Saxton was —they went down to Cuba again. This time Simonovich had only one passenger for them, again Chinese, but he was a lucrative one because he was to be taken all the way to California. Again the flyers put down successfully at Fort Lauderdale, climbed into the station wagon, and set out. By February 1 they were peacefully driving along U.S. 80 in California, congratulating themselves, when they ran into a Border Patrol roadblock, regularly posted there to intercept Mexican wetbacks on their way to Imperial Valley. That was the end of their career as smugglers. On May 4, 1951, in Federal Court in Los Angeles, Morgan got a two-year prison sentence and Robinson an eighteen-month one.

Meanwhile the Immigration Service had become engaged in what it hoped would be, if not a conclusive set-to with Simonovich, at least a campaign of massive retaliation against addlepated flyboys. During the middle of February a Washington, D.C., printer with a wide acquaintance reported to the Immigration Service that an aviating friend of his was trying to find venture capital for a Cuba-to-Florida alien-smuggling project. The service chiefs studied their personnel list and decided that a tall, tough, handsome agent named Jay Stanley Hartzell was a likely looking capitalist for this kind of venture, and sent him off to the printer's office to confer with the aviator whose name, let's say, was Billy Clancy. According to Hartzell's subsequent testimony in court, Clancy's notion, which he freely confided to Hartzell, who gave a persuasive impersonation of a knowing and carefree gambling man, was pretty much the same as Murphy's or Saxton's or Morgan's and Robinson's. He proposed going down to Florida, lining up suitable aircraft and landing fields, and then making connections in Cuba. The only real difference between Clancy's scheme and those of his predecessors was that Clancy, not being quite so slapdash a character as they, insisted on a certain amount of careful preliminary organization. Hartzell expressed himself as being delighted with Clancy's plans, and more than willing to second them. On March 2 the pair of them went down to Deland, Florida, for consultations with a flying friend of Clancy's who, presumably, was familiar with the ins and outs of alien smuggling. These consultations, involving such questions as the best routes from Cuba to Florida, suitable types of aircraft, and whether or not to build extra fuel capacity into a plane or risk refueling stops, occupied two or three days. Not all the points, though, were settled to Clancy's satisfaction, and his friend advised him that for further information he should interview still another flyer in Miami. Thereupon Clancy and Hartzell went to Miami and spent another few days discussing the same subjects with Clancy's friend's friend, also with inconclusive results. Finally Clancy's friend's friend said that he knew just the man to consult, and introduced them to Murphy, who had only recently been paroled. Murphy wanted five hundred dollars before saying a word. Clancy and Hartzell didn't have any such sum, but they agreed Murphy's advice was worth purchasing, so they went back north to raise money. A week later they returned to Miami. Hartzell said ruefully that he had had no luck with fund raising in Washington, but Clancy, who had been in New York, had managed to gather the necessary cash, which he gave Murphy. In return Murphy turned over some marked maps of Cuba, southern Florida and the ocean in between, told them how and where to find Simonovich in Havana, and recommended that they purchase their own plane and modify its fuel capacity according to their needs. Renting planes was too risky, he warned them. The next day Clancy and Hartzell went to Havana and saw Simonovich. Simonovich, as usual, was happy to make the acquaintance of an American flyer and his partner, and assured them that there was plenty of business to be done. Clancy and Hartzell returned from Havana to Deland where they agreed to purchase a twin-engined Cessna plane from Clancy's friend for eighteen hundred dollars. That contract necessitated a second money-raising tour of the north. Again Hartzell failed as a financier and Clancy succeeded. On March 23 Clancy went back to Havana to tell Simonovich of his purchase, to inspect possible landing fields in Cuba and to arrange a system of telephonic communication between Havana and Deland. He then returned to Deland where he and Hartzell spent a couple of weeks working on the plane, and waiting word from Simonovich. None came—Simonovich, it seems, had taken sick about that time—and since neither partner could afford to hang about indefinitely without income, Hartzell returned to Washington and his alleged gambling interests, and Clancy picked up a few flying jobs in Florida. In May Simonovich at last got word to Clancy that he was ready to go. Hartzell immediately went back south, and then to Havana, where he had a talk with Simonovich about the newest plans. Simonovich was supposed to have a passenger list ready on May 26, but he canceled it at the last moment. The same thing happened on May 30 and June 4. Then came another lull. Finally on July 9 Clancy went to Havana again, saw Simonovich again, and made plans again. July 11 was to be the date this time, and on that day Clancy and Hartzell took off from Deland. They had been in the air only a few minutes when engine trouble developed and they had to return to Deland. They spent the rest of the day tinkering with the plane, and took off again the following morning. This time they got as far as Miami before the engine started acting up. They put down at Opa Locka. In considerable distress they called in Murphy for advice. He examined the Cessna and told them that with that plane the whole idea was out of the question. However, he said, he knew a fellow who might be able to help them out.

The fellow, whom Murphy promptly produced, was a larcenous airline co-pilot who had been acting as the financial backer—since, for a wonder, he was gainfully employed—for an entirely separate group of Murphy-encouraged would-be smugglers. This group, which had been operating since June, consisted of the co-pilot, who had best be known as George Balch, a flyer and occasional embezzler named Wilfred Goddard, and the proprietor of a Tampa shooting gallery, known laconically as Slim. Slim was a government informer in his spare time, of which he seemed to have plenty, and it was in that capacity that he was taking part in the plot. Balch, Goddard and Slim had been conferring with Simonovich, surveying airfields and purchasing and repairing planes in much the same manner as Clancy and Hartzell had, and with an equal lack of results. Murphy felt that the two groups ought to join forces and, particularly, bankrolls; without pooling Clancy's New York backing and Balch's ready cash, he pointed out, neither combine would ever be able to afford a plane in decent repair. Clancy, however, wanted no part of this new arrangement. He went back to New York, muttering that he'd had it, and so Hartzell attached himself to the Balch-Goddard partnership. The plane he and Clancy had bought, some parts of which, at least, were in working order, was his ticket of admission. After several more false passes—once there was engine trouble again, and once Goddard got down to Cuba, ready to carry back a load, and was sent back home by Cuban airport officials because his papers weren't in proper order—definite and apparently foolproof arrangements were made for August 3. Goddard was to fly down to Veradero Airport in Cuba, meet Simonovich, who would have four passengers for him, and fly them back to Zephyr Hills Airport near Miami. The Border Patrol, which had been irritably waiting for months for this carefully infiltrated group to do something, prepared to greet Goddard at Zephyr Hills with every possible attention. Goddard, though, was scarcely the stuff of which sucessful conspirators are made. He got down to Veradera uneventfully enough on August 3, but once there, feeling that some official or other was looking at him askance, suddenly took fright, leaped back into the plane without even looking for Simonovich, and headed home. Carefully avoiding Zephyr Hills, he put down at the 20th Street Airport in Miami, went to a telephone booth and called the Border Patrol. He was willing to tell all, he said. That just about ended that story. Clancy had withdrawn from the plot. Murphy had never been terribly active. Hartzell was an Immigration Service undercover man. Slim was an informer. Now Goddard wanted to be an informer too. That left Balch as the only sincere, full-time felon around—except, of course, Simonovich. There didn't seem to be much point in waiting for any more developments. The patrol, of course, took a statement from Goddard, and then turned it over, together with voluminous reports from Hartzell and Slim, to the United States Attorney. Presently, on September 18, a grand jury indicted Clancy, Murphy, Goddard, Balch and Simonovich for conspiracy to smuggle aliens. (They never actually managed to smuggle any, so conspiracy was the only thing they could be charged with.) Murphy was arrested while watching the stock car races at Opa Locka on the 19th, Clancy in New York on the 20th, Balch at his home in Miami on the 21st, and Goddard in Miami on October 4. Simonovich, of course, was still in Cuba. The four defendants were arraigned on October 5, pleaded not guilty, and were let out on bail. It appeared to be still another case of mopping up silly American flyers while Simonovich, the untouchable, continued to bask in the Havana sun. Then came the affair's utterly incomprehensible denouement.

6 *Surprise!*

On Sunday morning, November 4, at a time when there was light but not yet sun in the eastern sky over Miami, a Border Patrol inspector named John Pilcher was awakened by the ringing of his bedside telephone. He lifted the receiver laboriously to his ear and uttered a thick, "Hello." A male, but otherwise unidentifiable, voice said, "Somebody you want real bad's going to be at Prospect Field right about sunup." "Who's this?" Pilcher asked irritably. The answer he got was the click of a receiver being replaced on a hook. It might have occurred to Pilcher that he was being set up for a particularly unlaughable practical joke, but gullibility under such circumstances was part of his job. He immediately telephoned his superior officer, Chief Inspector Rex Kelley. "What are we waiting for?" Kelley said. Pilcher thereupon plunged into the Border Patrol's undress uniform of an open-necked shirt, a pair of slacks and a straw hat, and took off in the government Ford he had left parked outside his door. Picking up Kelley, similarly attired, en route, he drove to Prospect Field, which is about thirty miles north of his house, in just under half an hour. They arrived, as per instructions, at sunup. Prospect Field was a desolate, weedy place. One of dozens of unimportant practice landing strips that had sprouted in southern Florida during the war, it had been abandoned immediately thereafter, and in 1951 was simply three cracked concrete runways, separated by waist-high grass, at the end of an unpaved road that ran a mile or more through wilderness. Pilcher drove up and down the runways a couple of times without seeing a thing that anyone but a lepidopterist would have wanted. Then he stopped the car and got out to reconnoiter on foot, while Kelley took the wheel and followed him in low gear. After two or three minutes both men simultaneously caught sight of a frail figure wandering irresolutely along the edge of a runway. Kelley got there first in the car; Pilcher pounded up a few seconds later. It was the figure of a skinny little middle-aged man with a mane of gray hair, prominent cheekbones and widely spaced wistful eyes. He was wearing a faded blue work shirt with rolled up sleeves, a pair of frayed dungarees and sandals. He seemed completely bewildered. And as far as Pilcher and Kelley were concerned he was certainly bewildering, for he was, of course, Simonovich.

After Simonovich was duly arrested, arraigned and held in fifty thousand dollars bail—which he was unable to supply, since at the time of his appearance on Prospect Field he had precisely three dollars in Cuban money on his person—he was invited to tell his story. He persistently refused to, but he was voluble on the subject of how he happened to turn up on a deserted Florida landing strip at dawn on a November Sunday. He had been kidnapped, he said. On the previous morning, according to his account, he had been peacefully drinking coffee in a shop near his home in Havana when he was approached by three Americans. They pulled guns on him, and forced him to enter a car they had parked nearby and lie down on the floor. Then they taped his eyes, his mouth and his ankles, handcuffed his wrists, and took him to a room somewhere in the city where they kept him all day and some of the night. In the middle of the night they took him out to an airfield, put him in a plane, and took off. Once in the air they removed the tape and handcuffs and gave him coffee and sandwiches. A few hours later they put down at Prospect Field, pushed him off the plane, and took off again without even having cut the motors. Two or three minutes later the Border Patrol showed up and arrested him. However, Simonovich said, he had managed to get the description and registration number of the plane when it took off from Prospect after leaving him there. It was a twin-engined yellow or cream-colored Cessna, he said, number 55703. Furthermore, he said, it was quite clear to him that the Border Patrol, which had been persecuting him for years, was responsible for his abduction. Now this last charge, if it could have been substantiated, would have had grave consequences. However palpably guilty Simonovich may have been of the crimes with which he was charged, if his arrest had been illegally engineered by the Border Patrol, he would have had to be released. If, on the other hand, neither the Border Patrol nor any other law-enforcement agency had had anything to do with his arrival in the United States, his arrest was valid even though all the rest of the kidnapping story was true. Kidnapping is an FBI matter, and the FBI was immediately ordered to investigate Simonovich's story. There was precisely such a plane as the one Simonovich described, it was soon discovered, and it had been in Cuba on the day in question. The plane belonged to a young sport from West Palm Beach, the son of a prosperous automobile dealer there. This character, apparently for want of anything better to do, had cast himself in the role of volunteer righter of wrongs and defender of the American way, somewhat on the order of the Saint, perhaps. On several occasions he had offered his services to the Border Patrol, but there was no evidence that the offers had ever been accepted. Furthermore, the FBI was able to determine, Simonovich had seen both the young man and his plane several times before the fateful day in question, and so he would have had no difficulty in providing the description even if he had been delivered to Prospect Field by some entirely different aircraft. Finally, whatever case there was against the Border Patrol—or the young man from West Palm Beach, for that matter—broke down completely over the matter of the mysterious telephone call to Pilcher. It was a local, not a long-distance call. It clearly couldn't have been made by Simonovich's abductors—if any such people existed—since they must have been several thousand feet in the air at the time it was made. It was highly improbable that it could have been arranged for by the abductors before they took off from Cuba; the timing was too exact for that. How it was made, and by whom, continued to remain thoroughly inexplicable. Upon reviewing the FBI's findings, the U.S. judge sitting on the case concluded—with no visible reluctance—that the matter of Simonovich's appearance in this country was irrelevant to the charges against him, and ordered the prisoner and his four co-defendants tried forthwith on the conspiracy charges. The highlight of the trial, which lasted for a couple of weeks, was Hartzell's elaborate testimony about his life with the would-be smugglers. Clancy, Balch, Goddard and Murphy testified in their own behalfs. Simonovich continued to remain silent. The jury finally found Simonovich and Goddard guilty, and failed to agree on the guilt of the other three. Goddard was sentenced to one year in prison, Simonovich to two. Shortly thereafter Simonovich was arraigned on the charges growing out of his association with Saxton, and pleaded guilty. In May he was sentenced for these misdeeds to a stiff thirteen years in prison, the sentence to run concurrently with the previous two-year one. Meanwhile a re-trial of Clancy, Balch and Murphy had been held, and again there was a hung jury. These cases were pursued no further, and neither were the charges against Simonovich for his connection with Murphy's activities in 1948. In January, 1953, Murphy's body, wearing only shorts, was found floating in Lake Okeechobee. He had apparently been practising crash landings there with a certain lack of success.

Simonovich is now in the Federal penitentiary in Atlanta, and very likely will remain there for a good ten years more. Meanwhile, despite the fishiness of his arrest, it is pretty clear that no fundamental miscarriage of justice was perpetrated. Since that November Sunday, as far as the Border Patrol can tell—and that's a long way— there has been virtually no smuggling of aliens from Cuba into the United States. Simonovich was the right man.

PART FIVE

Salvatore Sollazzo

1 *Armed robber and tax evader*

Business success in the underworld, obviously, is a condition that is rarely attended by renown; a well-known crook is, almost by definition, an unsuccessful one, and that there is no shortage of unsuccessful crooks is a fact that can easily be established by a random count of crime stories in any day's newspaper. Even in this overcrowded field, though, there appears every so often an especially spectacular example of failure, one that seems to sum up, in the career of a single individual, all the ills that a person can bring upon himself. The most noteworthy recent case in point was a gullible, good-natured man named Salvatore Sollazzo. In 1948 Sollazzo, who was then forty-four years old, was living in ease in a four-hundred-and-fifty-dollar-a-month apartment in the Majestic on Central Park West at Seventy-second Street. He owned two jewelry manufacturing firms and was one of the country's most prosperous manufacturers of wedding rings. He had just married a beautiful young photographer's model. He had more than enough convivial friends. His work left him plenty of time for frequent visits to such congenial spots as Yankee Stadium, Belmont Park and the

Latin Quarter. He was happy, affluent and completely obscure. Three years later this same Sollazzo was in a spectacularly altered situation. One of his two firms had been auctioned off to satisfy his commercial creditors, and the other had been mortgaged to pay for legal defenses. Against the nonexistent remainder of his property the United States of America had filed liens totaling $1,138,-493.57 for unpaid income taxes and penalties, and a federal grand jury had indicted him for fraud in connection with his tax deficiencies. The United States Secret Service was in possession of evidence that implicated him in black-market dealings in gold to the amount of several million dollars. The United States Immigration and Naturalization Service was preparing an order for him to be deported to Italy, a country he had not seen since he was fifteen months old. He occupied a cell in the Tombs while he awaited trial on thirty charges of offending against the peace and dignity of the people of the State of New York. And he had become a celebrity.

Perversely, it was not Sollazzo's grave and profitable crimes against the United States that brought him fame, but the fact that, thirty times, he trespassed upon the peace and dignity of his fellow New Yorkers by flouting a state statute, almost unknown up to then, concerning the bribery of amateur athletes. He had paid nine basketball players from Long Island University and the College of the City of New York some twenty-seven thousand dollars to play badly in games on which he placed bets—bets that, again perversely, he had lost as often as he had won. By bringing, in the words of one judge, "disgrace on a great institution" (C.C.N.Y.), and being responsible for, in the words of another, "the corruption of youth at its very fountainhead," he made clear to the world that he was, in the words of a third, "a cool, calculating and cunning weasel," and so made himself celebrated. As one of his lawyers wrote in the course of an unsuccessful attempt to get the venue of the basketball trial changed from New York County, "News of the Korean War during the time that this 'scandal' was receiving public airing is hard to find in the newspapers. This story took precedence over any other single thing that happened in the world for a period of about three weeks."

Until Sollazzo tried to mastermind a few basketball games, he certainly gave no indication that he would some day be more engrossing than a war. He was born in Palermo, Sicily, on December 31, 1904, the fourth in a family of seven children. His father, Giochimo Sollazzo, was a jewelry maker and repairman. When Salvatore—or Tarto, as most people were to call him most of his life—was fifteen months old, the family emigrated and settled in Brooklyn, where the senior Sollazzo continued to work at his trade, starting in a small way in his home, then, as business improved, opening a shop on Fulton Street in downtown Brooklyn, and finally moving from there to even more desirable quarters on Nassau Street in downtown Manhattan. When he died in 1930 at the age of fifty-seven, the value of the business was appraised, with some precision, at $30,214.69. Tarto meanwhile had made normal progress through the public school system, graduating from P.S. 164 in 1919, and had then gone to work for his father. In 1926 he married and left his parents' home to live with his wife's family. In 1929 he became the father of a son who was christened Salvatore but has always been called Robert. When Giochimo Sollazzo died, Tarto was the fifty-five-dollar-a-week manager of the Nassau Street shop, a garrulous, extravagant, quick-tempered man, whose hairline was already moving back, whose fondness for his wife and son was no more and no less compelling than his desire to spend whatever evenings he could with the boys, whose efficiency as a workman was considerably diluted by his lack of perseverance and childlike belief in luck, and who obviously had no destiny other than to drift through life without making either himself or anyone else particularly happy or particularly sad.

The effect his father's death had on Sollazzo was apparently powerful because from then on, his life became unaccountably picturesque. The first thing he did, in collaboration with his brothers, was put the business into bankruptcy in less than a year. In this project the boys were favored, to be sure, by the economic environment of 1931, but even so their execution of it was markedly more efficient than anything else they had ever done. Thereupon Sollazzo took to peddling jewelry from door to door, obtaining his wares on memorandum, an arrangement, common in the jewelry trade, whereby the shipper gives the salesman goods on credit and agrees to take back whatever is not sold. He made an extremely poor living at it, and presently was arrested on a charge of selling some of his merchandise without paying for it. He managed to get this charge dismissed. Not long after that his wife discovered conclusively that the evenings he had been spending with the boys had been devoted to other activities than shooting pool and singing facetious songs. She promptly declined to have anything further to do with him, and he moved back with his mother. Six months after that he participated, as an unarmed lookout, in an otherwise armed attempt to rob a jewelry firm on West Thirty-first Street. He was arrested, indicted, tried, and convicted of armed robbery and was sentenced to a stiff seven-and-a-half-to-fifteen-year prison term. Between his arrest for robbery and his trial he had been arrested a second time for the illegal sale of jewelry obtained on memorandum, but again the charge was dismissed.

In Sing Sing, where he served most of his time, Sollazzo was a docile prisoner, and in five years, the absolute minimum, he was given his parole. His wife still refused to have any dealings with him, and he returned to his mother's home in Brooklyn. A brother who was still in the jewelry business gave him a job as a salesman at fifteen dollars a week plus commissions. Prison had apparently steadied him somewhat. He worked hard, contributed money each week to the support of his wife and son and adhered faithfully to all the parole regulations. After a few months he improved his salary by changing employers, and by another change soon improved it still more. By the beginning of 1940 he had acquired sufficient capital to go into business for himself as Francine Manufacturing Jewelers, Inc., makers of wedding and birthstone rings. He worried along with Francine for three years, making an uneven but never substantial living. In 1943, to his own surprise as well as the rest of the trade's, he suddenly made a killing in platinum. What happened was that Sollazzo, never one to let his credit rating lie fallow, had been buying platinum on credit for speculative purposes. Neither then nor subsequently, however, did he have any talent as a speculator. When it became time to pay up the value of his holdings had decreased somewhat instead of rising. Instead of getting out fast, he renegotiated the deal by doubling his holdings. After one or two more such renegotiations he found himself owing some sixty thousand dollars for platinum which was worth no more than fifty-five thousand, leaving a gap that represented approximately a year's income. Then, without warning, platinum was declared a scarce war material, its use was banned in the manufacture of jewelry, and a black market instantly developed on which the value of the metal almost doubled. Instead of being five thousand dollars in debt, Sollazzo found himself more than fifty thousand to the good. By dangling his large supply of platinum before the dazzled eyes of potential purchasers of wedding and birthstone rings, Sollazzo was able to multiply his customers many times, and with the profits from the platinum he was able to expand Francine's facilities and, in 1944, to set up a second company, Supreme Wedding Ring, in the names of some friends. Soon he was the fourth largest wedding ring manufacturer in the country, employing eighty-odd people and doing a gross business of a million and a half dollars a year.

However, good fortune couldn't have fallen upon a man less able to bear it. Twelve years before Sollazzo had been driven to crime by poverty; now wealth was to have the same effect. The first thing he did upon coming into money, naturally, was to carefully swindle the government out of most of the income tax he owed it. He managed this by changing identity when dealing with the out-of-town concerns which provided him with more than half his business. Appropriating the names of Anthony Antonucci and H. Schwartz, two jewelry manufacturers of his acquaintance who were conveniently serving overseas with the armed forces, he arranged to have his out-of-town customers send their checks, payable to Antonucci or Schwartz, to a post office box. He then turned them over to a female employee who also, at the time, was filling the gap his wife's obduracy had left in his private life. He had prevailed upon this young woman to set up five bank accounts in the three fictitious names of Sylvia Weber, Sylvia Pomerantz and Mary Juliano. She deposited the checks in these accounts and, when they had cleared, withdrew the money in cash and gave it to Sollazzo. His New York customers, with whom he could not pose as Antonucci or Schwartz, he persuaded to pay him in cash or in checks payable to cash, and these checks also were Webered, Pomerantzed or Julianoed. He also maintained several accounts of his own under various names, into which he put some of the bundles of currency he was getting. In the five years from 1943 through 1947, according to the Intelligence Unit of the Bureau of Internal Revenue and the United States Tax Court, Sollazzo failed to pay $596,229.38 in taxes. His biggest year was 1944 when he declared an income of roughly $29,000 and paid a tax of some $12,000, whereas he should have declared $266,000 and paid $223,000.

2 *Gold smuggler*

Sollazzo's parole expired in 1947, and this event appears to have been a critical one in his life. Until then, except for such conventional, even semi-respectable, wrongdoing as cheating the United States Government, he had been leading an obedient life. In such crucial matters as "being in his home at a reasonable hour at night as determined by his parole officer," "not leaving the State of New York without the written permission of his parole officer," and "abstaining from the use of intoxicating liquors," he had been a model parolee. With the lifting of these embargoes he rapidly acquired a new personality which he was subsequently, and accurately, to describe as "the biggest sucker to hit Broadway in years." He began to frequent a number of night clubs where his tipping provoked admiration among the hat check girls. He acquired a new wardrobe, most of it custom and monogrammed. He bought season tickets at the Polo Grounds and Yankee Stadium, ringside seats for the Garden fights and clubhouse badges for Belmont, Jamaica and Aqueduct. He became a familiar of various mobsters, touts and skinny stiff-gaited young women who wore a great deal of mink and lipstick, and carried hatboxes. And he began to gamble. In his own words, uttered later under painful circumstances, he became "a diseased gambler, Your Honor. A diseased gambler just like a diseased narcotics user." To bookmakers he was a delight. He would bet as much as five thousand dollars on one baseball game or one horse race. Since he was poorly informed he could usually be depended on to pick a loser; since he was gullible he could easily be touted on to a loser if he accidentally happened not to pick one himself. On basketball alone, between 1948 and 1951, he lost a quarter of a million dollars. As perilous to his own well-being and as absurd to a dispassionate observer as this behavior was, it was also rather touching. Sollazzo was being a big shot in the only way he knew how.

Among the new acquaintances Sollazzo made at the start of this exuberant period was a tall, twenty-three-year-old dark-haired model from Philadelphia, a divorcee named Jean Wright. He was smitten and so, it seems, was she. During 1947, with the permission of the Parole Board, he had obtained a divorce on the statutory and sensible ground that his wife had refused to live with him for sixteen years. He had agreed to give her a hundred dollars a week and had set up a fifteen thousand dollar trust fund for Robert. He and Miss Wright were married on July 1, 1948. Being the spouse of a strikingly attractive young woman was obviously a substantial triumph for a middle-aged, Italian-born ex-convict. Certainly it did not diminish his yearning for notoriety. Although they started housekeeping modestly enough in a three-room $125-a-month apartment on East Fortieth Street, in less than a year the Sollazzos had transferred their home to a $450-a-month job at the Majestic on Central Park West. With such an eye-catching companion to exhibit, Sollazzo, of course, continued to frequent the public places where he was most likely to be conspicuous. And to a constantly increasing extent he bet. Already he had reached the stage at which he needed a big killing merely to get even. He was even finding that the proceeds from his business, large as they were (being tax-free), were not large enough to support his bookmakers. He began to divert gold into the black market.

The black market in gold which flourished from 1946 to 1950 was in several ways a unique criminal phenomenon. Ever since 1934, when Congress passed the Gold Reserve Act in order to prevent the nation's gold reserves being drained by people who feared the paper obligations they held were worthless, it had been illegal for a private citizen to own fine gold in unfabricated form except for what the act calls "industrial, artistic or professional" purposes. Until after the war the act was virtually self-enforcing, principally because the inflexible price of thirty-five dollars an ounce that the Bureau of the Mint set on gold was too high to tempt anyone to purchase the metal illegally. The economic disruption that followed the war in most of the world changed this situation radically by making domestic gold policy an acute international problem. For one thing, post-war currency palpitations in Europe and Asia, and the spectacle of throngs of once prosperous but now destitute refugees, convinced large numbers of people that eighty or ninety dollars an ounce was a reasonable price for gold. For another most of the world's gold was now in the United States—or in the Soviet Union where, of course, it was completely inaccessible—and so an ambitious European or Asian hoarder could find nothing at home to hoard. And so, in a manner inexorable enough to warm the heart of the most devout laissez-faire economist, gold started finding its way out of the country in large quantities—as much as fifty million dollars a year according to some guessers. The beginning of this unprecedented racket caught the authorities pretty much off guard. The Customs Service had never before been much afflicted with wrong-way smugglers. The Secret Service was undermanned and fully occupied with its other many duties. The cast of characters involved in diverting the gold was an entirely new one, consisting largely not of known professional criminals but of the regular personnel of the jewelry business whose pasts were spotless and whose morals, presumably, were irreproachable. And to understand the jewelry trade itself, which, even when conducted legally, is indescribably chaotic, took no small amount of study.

There is no General Motors or Alcoa in jewelry. Everyone is a small operator; competition is excruciatingly fierce, and a large part of the trade lives, and always has, on "angles." The elaborately pyramided edifices of credit and security that are constructed in the trade are even greater architectural marvels than the small-loan systems that are found in boys' boarding schools. And by many jewelers a man who wanted to sell a fifty-thousand-dollar diamond necklace for five thousand dollars would be regarded without suspicion even if he wore a mask and carried a revolver in one hand and a set of skeleton keys in the other. From the trade's point of view, therefore, black marketing gold did not require an ethical revolution. It was just another angle, more lucrative than most, and easier to manage. All a jewelry manufacturer had to do was to purchase daily from the United States Assay Office or a refiner licensed by the Bureau of the Mint the amount of gold to which he was entitled by his own mint license—Sollazzo, as owner of Francine and Supreme, was permitted to hold 160 ounces at a time—make false entries in his books indicating that he had manufactured a batch of ring settings, say, for a fictitious customer in Duluth, and then turn the gold over at a handsome premium, to a black marketer. Although the Bureau of the Mint was supposed to subject all the books, vouchers, bills, cancelled checks and other papers of its licensees to severe scrutiny, and, if these papers appeared out of order, ask the Secret Service to conduct a general investigation, the Bureau's personnel and procedures were simply not adequate to cope with the mass of detail involved. Sollazzo, for example, committed an egregious violation of the Bureau's rules by incorporating Supreme under a dummy name when he, in fact, owned it, but this particular misdeed did not come to light for seven years.

With very few exceptions the people in the jewelry trade did not physically smuggle the gold out of the country. They merely made it available to people who did. In the complex and cumbersome job of spiriting the gold past Customs, a wide variety of techniques was used, most of them well-worn. Double-bottomed suitcases, metal bedposts, hollowed-out books, the cartridge loops in hunting jackets, girdles with inner linings and elevator heels all played their traditional parts. (One character, who overestimated the power of his thigh muscles, was detained as he was about to board a Paris-bound plane when a Customs man observed that he could barely lift his feet to mount the stairway.) One man carefully wrapped some rolled gold in aluminum foil to simulate salami; another clapped a sack between his shoulder blades and pretended to be a hunchback; several presumably pregnant women were actually carrying bullion under their hearts. Probably the favorite method of getting gold overseas, though, was in automobiles, since an automobile could carry more pounds than a person could ounces. Every conceivable part of a car was used by one smuggler or another: Under the fenders, inside the gas tank, inside the transmission, coated with grease in the tool box, under the floor boards, in the upholstery and anywhere else that might occur to anyone.

Sollazzo, of course, did not participate in any such imaginative and colorful activities. There is no evidence, in fact, that he had any specific knowledge of—or, for that matter, interest in—what happened to the gold after he had turned it over to one of the several black market jobbers of his acquaintance. He simply went to the shop each working morning; determined by telephone what the day's quotation was on black market gold; sent an errand boy to pick up his 160 ounces at a refinery and deliver them to a jobber; spent an hour or two scrambling his books, and then went to the ball game. Each week he would keep a hundred ounces or so to make plausible rings with, but he cut down his working force so drastically that he couldn't have used all the gold he was entitled to for legitimate commerce even if he had wanted to. Since he received a profit on the black-market gold that hovered around three and a half dollars an ounce, he was in the pleasant position of making something like twenty-five hundred dollars a week, tax free, as he sat in the ball park.

The only part of Sollazzo's share in the racket that wasn't routine and drab was the expensive method he devised of making his guilty riches look innocent. He employed, as secretary-treasurer of Francine, and as bookkeeper for both Francine and Supreme, a young man who had never kept a book in his life. Almost every morning, after the gold had been sold and Sollazzo was in possession of a thick packet of cash, he would scribble a list of the names and addresses of fictitious out-of-town jewelry concerns. He would give the cash and the list to the bookkeeper and the bookkeeper would go to the Railway Express office on East Forty-fifth Street and buy American Express money orders payable to Sollazzo by the firms on the list. During the height of his operation the purchase of money orders cost Sollazzo some sixteen thousand dollars a year, but this outlay enabled him to avoid the suspicion that large cash bank deposits would have provoked. The carefully invented names and addresses looked ornamental on his books, too, in case mint inspectors ever got mildly inquisitive. The entire black market in gold, of course, was built on the optimistic assumption that mildly inquisitive was all that any inspector would get. Once the authorities' curiosity sharpened up a little, the market collapsed.

3 Basketball fixer

Not even black market money could bring Sollazzo happiness. The more he made the more he gambled. The more he gambled the more he lost. And the more he lost the more he gambled. It was a conventional performance. In October, 1949, on his tour of night clubs, he made a new acquaintance, one Eddie Gard, a player on the Long Island University basketball team. Gard, the son of a Brooklyn doll manufacturer, was a junior at L.I.U., which he was attending on an athletic scholarship after having been seasoned for half a year at a prep school at the expense of some of the university's loyal supporters. Despite the pains that had been taken to make him feel welcome at L.I.U. he had successfully escaped infection by the old school spirit. As a freshman he had unreluctantly become part of a cabal, organized by a former star player, Jackie Goldsmith, to doctor the scores of games for the benefit of any gambler willing to pay for such service, and he had seen no reason to change his ways in subsequent years. When he met Sollazzo he had, by virtue of the commercial acumen he had displayed during the two previous seasons, taken over management of the business from Goldsmith, and was able to deliver an attractive package consisting of himself and two other regular players, Dick Feurtado and Adolph Bigos, to anyone with sufficient funds. Gard did not offer to lose games; that he would have regarded as improper. He merely proposed to shade their outcome in a delicate and artistic way, a procedure made possible by certain conditions peculiar to basketball betting. To a much greater degree than with most athletic contests, the outcome of basketball games is predictable: The favorite usually wins. A bookmaker who laid odds on basketball games, therefore, would either have to make those odds so lopsided that bettors would seek new outlets for their venture capital, or else, a good part of the time, he would pay out more money than he took in. Consequently all bets on basketball are even-money bets under the terms of which one of the teams is favored by a specified number of points—the difference, or "spread," between the loser's score and the winner's. If, for example, a team is favored by ten points and wins by only nine, the bettors who wagered against it collect. What Gard undertook to do in behalf of his clients was to win games by less than the point spread if L.I.U. was the favorite, and to lose by more if L.I.U. was the underdog.

Although Sollazzo had his first conversations with Gard in October, it was not until three months later that he made final arrangements to subsidize L.I.U. players. The delay, undoubtedly, was caused by a wrangle over terms, which was ultimately settled in Gard's favor, and in such a way as to substantiate Sollazzo's boast about his status as a sucker. (There was no reason, after all, for Gard to switch from his original backers to Sollazzo except that Sollazzo was willing to pay him more.) The contract was ratified during the first week of January, 1950, at a meeting attended by Sollazzo, Gard and Bigos in a room in the King Edward Hotel on West Forty-fourth Street. Sollazzo was to pay each player a thousand dollars a game, and as a bonus for signing up he then and there gave each of them a hundred dollars. The first game to which the arrangement applied was played in Madison Square Garden on January 17, between L.I.U. and North Carolina State. L.I.U. was favored, so Sollazzo put his money on North Carolina State. Gard, Bigos and Feurtado did their work so well that they lost the game 55-52. The following day Sollazzo gave three thousand dollars to Gard, and Gard passed a thousand dollars on to each of his conspiring teammates. Sollazzo had bet six thousand on the game so he made a profit of almost three thousand, a large sum for one night's work, it is true, but one that, in view of the size of the investment and the obvious human fallibility of subsidized college athletes, might have seemed to many sure-thing gamblers to be not large enough. In addition Gard, when he collected the money, imparted news. In the locker room after the game Sherman White, the team's center and most glittering star, had bitterly reproached Gard, Bigos, and Feurtado for the inferior quality of their play. It was Gard's opinion that the whole scheme would collapse unless White was cut in, an addition of thirty-three and a third per cent to the payroll. Sollazzo assented and Gard immediately invited White to Sollazzo's apartment for dinner. Gard had already become a familiar figure at the Majestic where he was known to the building employees and Sollazzo's servants as "Mr. Logan.") White, whose intelligence quotient was listed as eighty-two, and who had a record as a juvenile offender, had been graduated from Dwight Morrow High School in Englewood, New Jersey, 230th in a

class of 263. A number of people connected with Duquesne University—a power in the basketball world—
would have liked to see him play basketball there, but the
admissions board had been unable to stomach his academic qualifications. He had been admitted to Villanova,
and he had left that institution after his first half year's
grades of two Cs, two Ds and an F had been posted.
Thereupon L.I.U. snapped him up, and at L.I.U., in
the words of General Sessions Judge Saul S. Streit, "In
some miraculous manner, despite the demands made by
a severe basketball playing schedule, and daily practice
. . . he showed 'remarkable scholastic improvement.'"
This may have been due to the courses he took. In his
senior year, for example—he was a junior when he first
dined with Sollazzo—his academic program consisted of
Physical Education, Public Speaking, Music Seminar, Oil
Painting and Rhythms and Dance. White was not hard to
corrupt.

Sollazzo and the L.I.U. players cooperated at least twice
more that season, on a game with the University of
Cincinnati on February 24, which L.I.U. lost 83-65, and
on a game with Syracuse University on March 11, which
L.I.U. lost 80-52. Although he won money both times,
each game cost him four thousand dollars in salaries, plus
various elaborate meals for the players in restaurants and
at his home and a more than occasional ten- or twenty-
dollar bill for "carfare." That summer Gard, White and
another L.I.U. player, LeRoy Smith, got jobs at Grossinger's Hotel in the Catskills as "waiters," which meant that
they spent most of their time playing basketball on the
hotel team, a practice that apparently had no effect on
their standing as amateurs. The Sollazzos spent a week or
two at Grossinger's, and Sollazzo had a number of conver-

sations with Gard about the 1950-51 season. Neither
Feurtado nor Gard were any longer eligible for the team,
although they were still in school, because they had
played on it as freshmen and three years of intercollegiate
competition are all that are permitted any athlete. Gard
kept control of the fixing operations, however; though he
could not longer command a cash price, he could, with his
inside knowledge of what was going on, bet very successfully—especially since he had no payroll to meet. Reflect-
ing on future operations, he concluded that White and
Bigos alone would not be able to do a thorough job for
Sollazzo, and he suggested that Smith be signed up. The
job of enrolling Smith was given to White, who roomed
with him at a Brooklyn Y.M.C.A. during the school year.
Smith was so flattered that White should consider him
worthy of joining the inner circle that he agreed to do it
at half price.

Meanwhile Gard, a youth in whose bosom the spirit of
mercantile enterprise throbbed unceasingly, was extend-
ing his connections. During the summer he had occasion to
exchange views with Ed Warner, co-captain of the
College of the City of New York basketball team, who was
a high-scoring waiter at another Catskill hotel, Kline's
Hillside. The City College team was the talk of the basketball world at the time. After completing a season of play
that had been generally successful but by no means spectacular, it had gone on to win both of the major post-sea-
son intercollegiate tournaments, the National Invitation
and the National Collegiate Athletic Association, a feat
that had never before been accomplished and that had
induced practically every sports writer in the land to describe the team with the word "Cinderella" used as an
adjective. One reason for C.C.N.Y.'s less than perfect rec-

ord during the regular season had been that two of the players—Al Roth and Ed Roman, who was now the other co-captain—had on several occasions shaved points in behalf of a gambler unconnected with Sollazzo. (Roman was something of a phenomenon among the corrupt basketball players in that there was no question at all about his bona fides as a college student. He was a scholar of Phi Beta Kappa caliber.) Warner did not know what Roth and Roman had been doing in 1949-50 until Gard, a high school friend of Roth's, told him, as a powerful argument in favor of Warner's doing the same thing in 1950-51. Warner said he didn't think he was interested and Gard, who detected a certain lack of conviction in that reply, was content to let the idea simmer in Warner's mind for the time being. It was an active summer for Gard. He also found time to introduce Sollazzo to a family friend who was a basketball referee. Sollazzo, running faster and faster on the treadmill, wanted to persuade the man to influence the results of some of the professional basketball contests he refereed by calling so many personal fouls against the star players of the favored team that they would be ruled off the court. It was a project of extremely dubious practicality—for one thing referees are in enough trouble with the customers when they confine themselves to an honest enforcement of the rules—and it proved to be a totally profitless one for Sollazzo.

Through the early fall of 1950 Sollazzo was a far from happy man. He knew that Internal Revenue agents were examining his income tax returns and he had reason to believe that he would soon be called upon for explanations he would be unable to make. He was losing a good deal of money on the unfixable game of baseball and on horse racing which, if not precisely unfixable, was far beyond his power to fix. His income from illegal sales of gold continued to be large, but there were indications that the overseas demand was slackening and that the price would soon drop. He was relying heavily on the basketball season to square him, and even that prospect gave him qualms. In well-informed circles L.I.U. was becoming known as a notorious "dump" team. He feared that these circles would spread widely in the coming season if it lost or barely won many of its games, since it was clearly a team of exceptional strength. What bothered him about this prospect, characteristically, was not the idea of being caught and punished for "corrupting youth at its very fountainhead," but the thought that if the Broadway bookmakers became persuaded that L.I.U. was dumping, they would no longer accept his bets against the college. He urged Gard to instruct the players to exceed the point spread instead of shaving it, a course of action that would both astound the bookmakers and be legal—since it obviously couldn't be a crime for a team to try to win by a greater margin than was expected of it. As Gard pointed out to him, though, "going over" the points was a plan that was much easier for a wedding-ring manufacturer to devise than for a basketball team to execute. He was forced to accept this dictum from his technical expert.

On December 2, 1950, L.I.U. played Kansas State in the Garden. The original quotations on the game had made L.I.U. an eight-point favorite, but by the time Sollazzo called his bookmaker the points had gone down to six, and when he said he wanted to bet seventy-five hundred dollars against L.I.U. all he could get was four. He spent a nerve-wracking evening at the Garden watching the L.I.U. players wrestle with their consciences. Finally business integrity triumphed over athletic skill and L.I.U. floundered to a 60-59 victory. Of the seventy-five he won, Sollazzo had to pay the players twenty-five hundred.

Gard had not forgotten about C.C.N.Y. and Ed Warner, who, with the chance to earn money right at hand, now proved to have fewer scruples than he did under the blue Catskill skies. Gard also had some talks with Warner's teammate and friend, Floyd Layne. As a result it had been possible for Sollazzo to enter into an expensive deal with the City College players. As with L.I.U., Sollazzo wanted C.C.N.Y. to go over the points, and for five hundred dollars apiece Warner and Layne had agreed to try in a game against Brigham Young. They did their best but their fellow players, Roman and Roth, presumably in behalf of some other gambler, played so poorly that City College lost the game and Sollazzo lost five thousand dollars. Clearly things couldn't continue that way. Warner had a heart-to-heart talk with Roman who consulted Roth and then announced that they would work for Sollazzo on two conditions: That they go under the points, not over, and that they get from a thousand to fifteen hundred dollars a game—depending on how large a bet Sollazzo was able to place—for doing it. This arrangement took devastating effect on the night of December 9th, when C.C.N.Y., playing Missouri at the Garden, was favored by fourteen points and lost by seventeen. Sollazzo, however, barely won more than he needed for expenses since the bookmakers were beginning to get leery of his bets. From then until the middle of January the players of both teams continued to play as badly as possible, but their efforts did Sollazzo little good. On December 7 L.I.U., the favorite, beat Denver 58-56, which was under the points, but Sollazzo had only managed to get six thousand down on the game, most of which was consumed by his expenses. He did even worse on Christmas when L.I.U. played Idaho. Again L.I.U. won by a mere two. This time, though, Sollazzo couldn't even bet enough to cover his expenses, so queasy were the bookmakers about both him and L.I.U. On December 28 he won a little money when City College, a seven-point favorite, lost to Arizona, 41-38. The same night L.I.U. played Western Kentucky. This time the players agreed to go over the points, which were ten. Until the last few minutes of play L.I.U. led by a large score, then the team went into an inexplicable decline and finally won by a mere seven. Since he was betting in favor of L.I.U. instead of against it as he usually did, Sollazzo was able to invest ten thousand dollars in this game. The result made him certain, not that going over the points was, as Gard had said, an intricate matter, but that Gard and the players were doing business with someone else. By then, though, he was, as he later said, so "broke and bewildered" that he felt he had no choice but to try again. On January 4 L.I.U. was a seven-point favorite over Bowling Green. On the basis of his ten-thousand-dollar loss, Sollazzo was able to get some money down against L.I.U. on this one, and he was horrified to watch the team, sparked by White and Smith, roll up an enormous lead during the first half. In the dressing room between halves, though, Bigos denounced his two teammates as welchers, and during the second half, by a supreme show of ineptness, they managed to let Bowling Green creep up to within six points. Their performance was so transparent that the spectators booed and shouted such cynical comments as "Hey, Smitty, what's the points tonight?" Sollazzo became definitely alarmed and hurriedly left before the game was over. As he said later, "They literally stunk the place out."

Shortly after this game Clair Bee, the L.I.U. basketball coach—who had also recently been promoted to vice-president of the university—received an anonymous letter accusing Bigos, White and Smith of being in on a fix. He raised the question with the players and they, of course, denied everything. However the letter, coming so soon after the open criticism of their play against Bowling Green, thoroughly frightened them and they resolved to do no further dumping. They neglected to make this decision clear to Sollazzo, though, and on January 16th, under the impression that they were working for him in the game against Duquesne, he bet as heavily as he could on Duquesne, which was quoted as a six-point underdog. It wasn't until the game was actually under way that he was told the fix wasn't in. That night the L.I.U. team, apparently relieved at playing with unanimous determination to win for a change, rolled up an 84-52 score against Duquesne. Two days later the news broke that Junius Kellogg, an outstanding member of the Manhattan College basketball team, had been approached by gamblers—who had no connection at all with Sollazzo —with a proposal to dump the Manhattan-De Paul game on January 16. The uproar caused by this revelation thoroughly persuaded the L.I.U. players that they had adopted a prudent course in playing to win.

The Duquesne disaster, in fact, finished Sollazzo as a member of the sporting set. He had been touted on the Manhattan-De Paul game and had lost heavily on it when Kellogg elected to remain honest. A few nights before, the City College team, following orders, had lost to Boston College 63-59, but he had only been able to bet twenty-five hundred dollars on it, which was a thousand dollars less than he owed the players. (Warner had a bad knee that night and didn't play, so he was entitled to only five hundred.) L.I.U.'s spasm of virtue against Duquesne brought his season's net losses on basketball to seventy-five thousand dollars. So broke was he that he paid the City College players only fourteen hundred dollars for their work against Boston College, and this so disillusioned them that they, too, decided to play to win in the future.

4 *Pauper, prisoner and undesirable alien*

Once the two teams returned to grace, the only means of resolving his difficulties left to Sollazzo was getting caught. That final task he performed promptly and methodically. Since December the New York District Attorney, Frank S. Hogan, and his assistant in charge of racket investigations, Vincent A. J. O'Conor, had been trying to work up evidence about basketball fixes. Both the telephones and the persons of a number of suspicious characters had been under surveillance with, for the first few weeks, inconclusive results. However, on January 10, two metropolitan sports writers brought Hogan a tip that Eddie Gard was worth watching, and O'Conor, to whom he passed the tip on, arranged at once for Gard to be included in the program. Thus he soon became aware that a person named Sollazzo existed. It was fortunate for the forces of law and order that Sollazzo owed the City College players twenty-one hundred dollars. In most other respects he had concluded his involvement with college basketball at almost precisely the moment that Hogan first found out about him. The exasperated efforts of the C.C.N.Y. people, via Gard, to collect the money they were owed, provided the District Attorney's detectives with the principal clues to Sollazzo's activities that they were able to assemble. The one other suspicious relationship that the detectives unearthed was between Gard and Sollazzo and a member of the New York University team named Harvey Schaff. Schaff was a boyhood friend of Gard's, whose ethics, but not whose talents, he shared. He had met Sollazzo at Grossinger's, where he, too, had been an all-star waiter. He knew what was happening at City College and L.I.U., and was anxious to make a similar arrangement at N.Y.U. Despite strenuous efforts he was unable to induce any teammates to share his views, and he was in no position to fix games single-handed. He did, however, continue to beg Gard and Sollazzo for a chance to make some fast momey, and he was partly appeased by various invitations to dinner and frequent donations of pocket money in twenty-five to fifty-dollar installments. He rapidly became a familiar figure to the detectives who were watching and listening to Sollazzo and Gard.

The evidence that was gathered for O'Conor was not of the sort that would lead to convictions. It consisted principally of embarrassed and opaque telephonic references to "squaring things" with "the uptown girls" (the City College players), to meetings between "that girl, Sally" (Sollazzo) and "that girl with the big nose" (Roman), and to the point spreads on various basketball games on which Sollazzo, despite the reluctance of almost every bookie of his acquaintance, continued to try to bet. The District Attorney's detectives were also able to observe a long, intense conference between Sollazzo and Roman one Sunday afternoon in a saloon on East Fifty-ninth Street, and a less solemn conversation between Sollazzo and Schaff in the bar of the Mansfield Hotel, following which the two went out and stood on the sidewalk while Sollazzo handed Schaff some money. What with these and other shreds of evidence assembled here and there, O'Conor decided to order Sollazzo, Gard, Schaff, Roman, Roth and Warner brought in for questioning. The maneuver was executed late on the night of Saturday, February 17, when the C.C.N.Y. team returned to New York after a game in Philadelphia. Hogan, O'Conor and two assistants questioned them all night in the District Attorney's office and some time close to dawn on Sunday, mainly as the result of letting the players hear tape recordings of their telephone conversations, enough admissions were obtained to arrest them all. Gard also started talking. Sollazzo didn't. On Monday, on the basis of what he had learned from the men already in custody, O'Conor summoned White, Bigos and Smith to a similar all-night session, at the end of which they also confessed and were arrested. Within a few days the players had surrendered almost all the money they had received from Sollazzo, some $26,430, all of which, except for $1,860 which the players successfully claimed were personal funds, was, according to law, put into the Police Pension Fund. Warner had $3,050 in a shoe box in the basement of the house he lived in. Roth had $5,060 in his mother's safe deposit box. Roman had $3,000 in the safekeeping of relatives. White had $5,500 taped to the back of a dresser drawer in his room at the Y. Smith had $1,030 in the toe of a shoe in the closet of the same room and $900 in his brother's safe deposit box. Bigos had $5,000 sewn into the lining of a sports jacket at his family's home in Perth Amboy, New Jersey. Layne, whom O'Conor didn't catch up with until February 28, had $2,890 in a flower pot in his home. Gard, who was subsequently described by Judge Streit as "quite the debonair night club man about town," had apparently spent most of his.

In incarcerating Sollazzo the New York District Attorney was only a very few weeks ahead of the United States Secret Service, which had also become interested in him through a series of happenings unrelated to basketball and entirely unknown to Hogan or O'Conor. On the morning of February 15 a man named Saul Chabot had delivered to Pier 90, North River, a 1950 two-door Buick sedan which he was planning to take with him to France on the Queen Elizabeth, sailing at one o'clock the following morning. That afternoon the pier checker began to prepare it for loading. In the course of attempting to empty the gasoline tank, he discovered that the rear end was so unusually low that he couldn't get at the drain plug. He informed one of the Customs inspectors on the pier of his problem, and the inspector summoned three expert car searchers from the Cargo Division of Customs. They found, in specially built compartments under the rear fenders, eighty-two packages, wrapped in black cotton cloth and tied with white string, which contained altogether 4,891.36 troy ounces of gold bullion worth $171,196.60, in the form of 164 Assay Office bars. Chabot was arrested that evening in his cabin on the ship. He turned out to be, incidentally, brother-in-law to a man who had been arrested several months before at a British airport with gold concealed in his baggage; he also turned out to be, according to his passport, a frequent trans-Atlantic traveler although his ostensible occupation was old-rag-and-bottle man and there was no evidence that his business was thriving. Chabot was of less interest to the Secret Service, though, than the gold bars. Each bar sold by the Assay Office is stamped with a number of things, including the seal of the United States, a serial number, its degree of fineness and its precise weight to the hundredth of an ounce. On the Chabot bars, as on almost all black market bars, the numbers had been obliterated. However the Assay Office laboratory is extremely proficient at deciphering obliterated numbers, and it presently determined that several of the bars had once been the property of Francine Manufacturing Jewelers, Inc., Salvatore Sollazzo, pres. A federal grand jury in the Southern District of New York had started an investigation of gold smuggling only a few weeks before, and was edified by this information. Through some active legwork by the Secret Service and through questioning a number of witnesses, including most of the employees at Francine and Supreme, the grand jury was able to establish that the gold had been purchased during the latter part of January from a Newark refiner and that in the case of at least one bar Sollazzo had personally supervised the obliteration of the numbers; the job done on that bar was an outstanding botch. The Secret Service even ran down the tongs with which the bar had been held when the attempt to efface the numbers was made—a complex piece of sleuthing since, by that time, the Francine equipment had been auctioned off to help pay Sollazzo's business debts and was scattered all over New York. In connection with the basketball case the District Attorney had subpoenaed all of Sollazzo's books and records, and he now turned over the relevant portions to the United States Attorney, who was thus able to establish Sollazzo's shenanigans with American Express money orders. The grand jury did not get around to indicting Sollazzo—and sixty-four others—for their gold dealings until August 1952, but in Sollazzo's case there was certainly no hurry. He was not hard to find, being held in the Tombs awaiting disposition of the basketball case for the first part of the period, and in Clinton Prison in Dannemorra, N.Y., working off his sentence for most of the rest of it.

The law, in its devastating undoing of Sollazzo, got off to a brisk start. On February 23, 1951, five days after his arrest in the basketball case, the Collector of Internal Revenue, acting partly on information the Bureau's Intelligence Division had dredged from Sollazzo's subpoenaed records, filed a $1,128,493.57 tax lien against him covering the five years from 1943 through 1947. On March 1 a second federal grand jury, beating the six-year statute of limitations by two weeks, indicted him for a tax fraud amounting to over $210,000 for the year 1944. (A year later, on February 29, 1952, he was indicted for tax frauds during 1945 amounting to more than $50,000.) The first indictments on the basketball case were handed down March 8, 1951; and on March 15, the Justice Department served a warrant on him calling for his deportation to Italy. Statistics on such a matter are not readily available but it is possible that Sollazzo, from February 18, to March 16, 1951, set an unbeatable record for running afoul of the law during a twenty-six-day period.

At this point the pace of the proceedings became more leisurely. The first case against Sollazzo to be disposed of was the basketball case. After maintaining his silence and innocence for several months, he finally pleaded guilty in July, 1951. Judge Streit didn't get around to sentencing him until November 20, doubtless because he was composing the famous sentence he then read, excoriating the manner in which institutions of higher learning recruited their basketball teams, and analyzing the greedy natures and lack of academic qualifications of most of the players whom Sollazzo had bribed. After exhaustively and convincingly demonstrating that the colleges themselves were as much to blame as anyone for the basketball scandals, he gave Sollazzo a whopping eight-to-sixteen year sentence, and Gard an up-to-three-year one. Most of the players got off with suspended sentences, although White, Warner and Schaff had to serve a few months each in the workhouse. Sollazzo was then carted off to Clinton Prison whence he was returned in March, 1953, for trial of the gold and income tax cases. A broken man, he pleaded guilty to everything, and Federal Judge Sylvester Ryan sentenced him to two years' imprisonment and ten thousand dollars fine for his gold dealings and one year's imprisonment and one thousand dollars' fine on each income tax count, all the sentences to run concurrently. Sollazzo's attorney tried his best to get reductions, and his various petitions, affidavits and other legal procedures kept Sollazzo in the House of Detention and out of State's prison until July. He's back in Clinton now. When he finishes his sentence there he will be turned over to the federal authorities, and when that term is completed, Immigration will take charge of him. He is, and will doubtless remain, penniless. To finance his defense he mortgaged Supreme, sold whatever personal property he had left including his wife's Cadillac and diamond ring, and induced his mother to give a second mortgage on her Brooklyn home. (His wife is now paying off the mortgage on Supreme, which she is operating as the Rite-Art Wedding Ring Co.) He owes the United States twelve thousand dollars in fines and more than a million in back taxes and penalties. The United States will probably never get its money, but the people of the State of New York certainly have a new hold on their peace and dignity.